↓↓↓

COOK IT NOW, SERVE IT LATER

↓↓↓

Other books by Maurice Moore-Betty:

Cooking for Occasions

*The Maurice Moore-Betty Cooking School
Book of Fine Cookery*

The Great Cooks Cookbook (Dessert Section)

Mary Poppins in the Kitchen
with P. L. Travers

The Maurice Moore-Betty Cookbook

COOK IT NOW, SERVE IT LATER

by

MAURICE MOORE-BETTY

THE BOBBS-MERRILL COMPANY, INC.
Indianapolis/New York

Library of Congress Cataloging in Publication Data

Moore-Betty, Maurice.
  Maurice Moore-Betty's Cook it now, serve it later.

  1. Cookery. I. Title. II. Title: Cook
it now, serve it later.
TX652.M665   641.5′55   81-66317
ISBN 0-672-52685-9   AACR2

Illustrations by Barbara Fiore
Designed by Jacques Chazaud
Manufactured in the United States of America

First printing

↡ ↡ ↡

To
E.C.P.A.
for many things

↡ ↡ ↡

⚡ ⚡ ⚡

ACKNOWLEDGMENTS

Barbara Reiss, my editor, gave me her usual guidance and encouragement.

Rosalyn Badalamenti contributed her meticulous editing and her understanding of my sometimes unorthodox methods.

And E. Ashworth showed his gift for deciphering my illegible handwriting when he typed the manuscript so accurately.

CONTENTS

$$\text{\textdownarrow}\text{\textdownarrow}\text{\textdownarrow}$$

INTRODUCTION

Eating is one of the great pleasures in life. It should be relaxed, with everyday troubles and woes left far from the table. The preparation of meals should be a joy and not a chore. With that in mind, I decided to put these menus together to enable you to prepare food ahead of time; to be at ease when the time comes to serve it; and, above all, to enjoy it—alone, with family, or with your friends.

Thanks to good refrigeration, efficient freezers, and the many labor-saving devices on the market, with a little time spent on study and much time on careful planning, it is possible to serve an elegantly simple dinner within an hour of getting home from the office. What a delight to be the guest of such a host or hostess! As a guest, I have found the most pleasure in dinner parties that have been prepared single-handedly and without any apparent effort. But anyone who has even the most rudimentary knowledge of the kitchen and what goes on there will know and appreciate all the time, energy, and planning that went into a delightfully comfortable evening.

Ever since I have had to fend for myself without kitchen help, I have stuck to hard and fast rules: Never complete a menu in one fell swoop—take it a step at a time over a period of time; plan something frozen, something chilled, and something ready for the stove top or oven. There are times when I set the table the evening before or early in the morning before leaving the house. Wine will be on the sideboard ready to be uncorked and suitable glasses in their proper place for cocktails. Canapés and cheese and such play no part in my planning, since I never offer anything to eat before going to the table. I prefer that my guests sit down with well-honed appetites, dulled neither by food nor by too much alcohol.

Twenty or thirty years ago in many households, the cook presented herself with pencil and paper to the head of the house to discuss the menus for the day. Today it is much more likely that the menu will be planned by a working wife or husband. The revolutionary way in which our lifestyle has changed (the scarcity of household help and the wherewithal to pay for it) means that we are compelled—unless our minds are made up to spend our lifelong eating-hours in restaurants—to learn the gentle art of cooking. To be free to choose what to eat and when to eat it is an indescribable freedom, a freedom that brings out the creative instinct inherent in all of us. It is revolutionary regenerative— mental and physical therapy.

Throughout this collection of "do-ahead" menus, I will advise you when to shop for the necessary ingredients, indicating the maximum time vegetables, meats, and other perishable ingredients will retain their freshness in the refrigerator; how far in advance a recipe may be prepared and whether it may be frozen; and how to prepare uncooked vegetables for storage.

The principle of the self-defrosting refrigerator is to remove moisture from inside the box. It is, therefore, of the utmost importance to store foods in airtight containers or wrap them securely in plastic wrapping; otherwise, they will quickly become dehydrated and worthless. This advice applies to freezing as well. Wrap foods securely, making the package thoroughly airtight. The sequence I follow for freezing and defrosting is one that works well. To freeze a food item, chill it in the refrigerator before wrapping. This ensures that ice crystals will not form. To defrost meat, transfer it to the refrigerator at least one day before it is to be cooked. Slow defrosting is the answer, bringing the meat to room temperature before cooking.

Advice to the beginner: Before attempting any of the following menus, first check your pantry and make a complete shopping list, drawing a line through those items that need not be purchased. Arrange the ingredients for each dish on a separate tray or baking sheet, together with the pots and pans you will need. This does away with last-minute searching for an elusive ingredient or utensil.

I have designed the menus in this book to suit most luncheon and dinner occasions. Generally the menus will comfortably accommodate four to six people. I have not specified the number of servings in a recipe, however, because it is really impossible to determine how many people a recipe will serve. The diners might well be four or six strapping young people sitting down to dinner after an afternoon of playing football or baseball. Or they might be three or four temperate eaters who are watching their weight. You must use your judgment and common sense, remembering my advice—make the servings small. In most cases, there should be no problem in doubling the recipes if you are entertaining eight or ten people. For cakes and soufflés, of course, do not double the recipe; make two cakes or two soufflés, instead.

You will also find menu suggestions for special occasions—such as major holidays like Thanksgiving, Christmas, and Easter—that guests and family love but that require anxious, exhausting hours in the kitchen for the cook who is not properly prepared and organized in advance. Other menus are given for buffets—lunch, dinner, or after-theater—and for festive events like a wedding breakfast and a birthday party. Each menu is designed to take the worry out of entertaining by doing the planning for you, so that you as the cook and host will enjoy your own parties as much as your guests will.

⅄ ⅄ ⅄

LIST OF MENUS

Zucchini Rapées with Sauce Tartare
Salmon en Papillote
Steamed Potatoes
Uncooked Almond Pudding
(page 23)

Chicken Mousse
Sole Eventail
Simple Green Salad
Brown Bread Ice Cream
(page 29)

Oxtail Soup
Petits Turbans of Sole
Simple Green Salad
Chocolate Truffles
(page 35)

⇟ ⇟ ⇟

Panache
Poached Salmon with Sauce Verte
Cucumber Salad
Lemon Curd and Whole Wheat Toast
(page 41)

⇟ ⇟ ⇟

Tomato Ice
Stuffed Striped Bass
Steamed Potatoes
Treacle Tart
(page 47)

⇟ ⇟ ⇟

Cucumber Mousse
Madras Shrimp
Orzo
Dolce Maddalena
(page 53)

⇟ ⇟ ⇟

⇟ ⇟ ⇟

Spinach Soup
Roulade of Crab
Simple Green Salad
Sabayon Frappé aux Pêches
(page 59)

⇟ ⇟ ⇟

Chick-Pea Salad
Crêpes de Volaille with Mornay Sauce
Ananas Glacés Orange
(page 64)

⇟ ⇟ ⇟

Deviled Crab
Chicken Marengo
Simple Green Salad
Apricot Mousse
(page 71)

⇟ ⇟ ⇟

3

↓↓↓

Low-Calorie Vegetable Soup
Chicken Breasts with Green Olives
Rice
Apple Crunch
(page 77)

↓↓↓

Antipasto with Italian Bread
Chicken Breasts en Papillote
Haricots Verts
Lime Sorbet
(page 83)

↓↓↓

Pannequet de Saumon Fumé
Virginia Baked Chicken
Simple Green Salad
Meringues
(page 89)

↓↓↓

⇟ ⇟ ⇟

Mousse of Ham
Chicken Florentine
Your Favorite Green Salad with Vinaigrette Dressing
Madeleines
(page 95)

⇟ ⇟ ⇟

Eggplant Caviar with French Bread
Chicken Cacciatore
Blueberry Grunt
(page 101)

⇟ ⇟ ⇟

Tapenade
French Bread and Unsalted Butter
Salad Argentine
Chocolate Mousse
(page 106)

⇟ ⇟ ⇟

⇓ ⇓ ⇓

Salad Romano
Roulade of Beef
Vegetable Mélange
Oranges and Cracked Caramel
(page 111)

⇓ ⇓ ⇓

Cream of Celery Soup
Pâté de Viande (Meat Loaf de Luxe)
Vegetable Salad
Pecan Meringue Torte
(page 117)

⇓ ⇓ ⇓

Smoked Haddock Muscatel in Aspic
Langue de Boeuf Fumée with Cranberry-Cumberland Sauce
Baked Apples
(page 123)

⇓ ⇓ ⇓

Mushrooms à la Grecque
Butterflied Leg of Lamb
Salad Bagatelle
Paris Brest
(page 129)

Coquilles St. Jacques
Shepherd's Pie
Valerie's Cold Orange Soufflé
(page 136)

Cold Cucumber Soup
Moussaka
Pear and Strawberry Compote
(page 142)

↓↓↓

Coleslaw
Cassoulet
Compote of Pears and Grapes
(page 147)

↓↓↓

Salad San Diego
Saucisson en Brioche with Sauce Madeira
Strawberries Escoffier
(page 153)

↓↓↓

Fish Terrine
Jambon Persillé
Tossed Green Salad with Vinaigrette Dressing
Baked Potato
Toasted Almond Parfait
(page 160)

↓↓↓

⇟ ⇟ ⇟

Creamed Smoked Haddock
Virginia Ham and Cumberland Sauce
Ambrosia
(page 166)

⇟ ⇟ ⇟

Fish Mousse
Escalopes de Veau Normande
Trifle
(page 171)

⇟ ⇟ ⇟

Mushroom Consommé
Collared Veal
Parsnip Purée
Rice Pudding de Luxe
(page 176)

⇟ ⇟ ⇟

⇟ ⇟ ⇟

Carrots Rapées
Vitello Tonnato
Frozen Coffee Mousse
(page 182)

⇟ ⇟ ⇟

Champignons sous Cloche
Curried Vegetables with Rice
Pineapple with Kirsch
(page 187)

⇟ ⇟ ⇟

Jellied Watercress Soup
Gnocchi Parisienne with Chicken Liver Sauce
Green Salad with Vinaigrette Dressing
Poires Noires
(page 193)

⇟ ⇟ ⇟

SPECIAL OCCASION MENUS

⇟ ⇟ ⇟

JULY FOURTH

Shrimp Scandia

Roast Chicken

Spaghetti Squash

Sabayon Frappé aux Pêches

(page 201)

⇟ ⇟ ⇟

THANKSGIVING

Pumpkin Soup

Casserole of Turkey and Chestnuts

Braised Celery

Purée of Carrots

Fresh Fruits

Mince Pies

(page 207)

⇟ ⇟ ⇟

CHRISTMAS DAY LUNCHEON

Oysters with Whole Wheat Bread and Lemon Wedges

Pheasant Casserole

Braised Celery

Plum Pudding with Hard Sauce

Fresh Fruits

(page 214)

⇟ ⇟ ⇟

NEW YEAR'S EVE

Creamed Smoked Haddock

Virginia Ham and Cumberland Sauce

Lima Bean Purée

Brown Bread Ice Cream

(page 221)

EASTER

Eggs Mimosa

Jambon Persillé

Green Salad with Vinaigrette Dressing

Trifle

(page 227)

WEDDING BREAKFAST

Poached Salmon with Sauce Verte

Butterflied Leg of Lamb

Vegetable Mélange

St. John's Iced Lime Soufflé

Bride's Cake

Champagne

(page 233)

⇟ ⇟ ⇟

BIRTHDAY PARTY

Jellied Watercress Soup
Gnocchi Parisienne with Chicken Liver Sauce
Your Favorite Green Salad with Vinaigrette Dressing
Birthday Cake
(page 241)

⇟ ⇟ ⇟

SUNDAY LUNCHEON

Cold Sliced Ham
Scrambled Eggs with Parsley
Pâté de Viande (Meat Loaf de Luxe)
Green Salad with Vinaigrette Dressing
Compote of Pears and Grapes
Nancy's Cookies
(page 247)

⇟ ⇟ ⇟

EVENING BUFFET

Panache
Salad Argentine
Poached Striped Bass
Trifle
Pineapple with Kirsch
(page 253)

⇟ ⇟ ⇟

⇟ ⇟ ⇟

AFTER-THEATER SUPPER
Zucchini Rapées with Sauce Tartare
Poached Salmon with Sauce Verte
Lemon Curd and Whole Wheat Toast
(page 259)

⇟ ⇟ ⇟

SUMMER BUFFET
Indian River Soup
Vitello Tonnato
Strawberries Escoffier
(page 264)

⇟ ⇟ ⇟

A PICNIC
Carrots Rapées
Virginia Baked Chicken
Chocolate Truffles
Fresh Fruits
(page 270)

⇟ ⇟ ⇟

↓↓↓

THE KITCHEN

A bright young couple, friends of mine, recently bought a large house not far from New York City. They came to me for advice: Should they remove the wall separating the dining room from the kitchen? And if they did, would it have an adverse effect on the resale value of the house? It took only a moment to answer. "Remove the wall and create a working, eating, and living area" was my advice. And as for the resale value, it will more than likely be increased. I continued: "The area should be functional, comfortable and beautiful." Household help has become increasingly scarce; and without it, preparing, toting food to another room, and serving it become a chore instead of a pleasure. The "cook" of the day, be it husband, wife, or any other member of the household, is separated for lengthy periods from guests or the rest of the family. By creating a space that will serve three functions, you are at the same time creating a sense of togetherness; and the heart of the house, the kitchen, beats once more.

The living and dining area of this complex should be comfortable, furnished with sofas, chairs, and tables that bear no resemblance to the conventional kitchen furniture we are accustomed to. A fireplace, if your climate calls for one, is an additional luxury. When planning the work area, keep the floor space down to the minimum. One should be able to stand in its center and take only one step in any direction to reach the stove, sink, or refrigerator. Both time and effort are saved.

Counter space comes next on my list of basic essentials. One cannot have too much flat surface to work on. Drop leaves attached to counters often solve this problem in small spaces. When not in use, they are lowered and are out of the way. Where possible have heat-resistant surfaces close to the stove and ovens.

Decide from the start on the very minimum amount of equipment you will need. Buy sparingly and wisely. Select pots and pans that are both heavy and easy to clean. Copper is all very well, wonderful to cook in, but almost a full-time job to keep clean. I prefer a heavy aluminum pan, treated so that it is impervious to acids, or well-designed heavy stainless steel. But no matter which you decide on, it should be heavy and should be capable of distributing heat evenly and retaining it. Start your collection with one 4-quart pan, then add a 2-quart and a 1-quart. Later buy an 8- to 10-quart enamel-coated cast iron pan for making stock: essential if, like me, you are a soup lover. Good pots and pans are expensive, but they will last a lifetime. A small nonstick saucepan for scrambling eggs and heating milk is almost a pleasure to clean.

Four knives should serve the needs of any cook: one 10-inch butcher's knife for chopping and heavy work, one 6-inch blade, and a small paring knife. A flexible slicing knife for hams and beef completes the set. Later, you can invest in a boning knife and one for slicing bread. A good knife is the cook's best friend. Care for it and use it for the purpose for which it was designed. Store knives in a wooden block with slots of varying size. If there are children around, put the block beyond their reach when it is not in use. Never cut paper or string or slice bread with your chopping and carving knives. Nothing will dull the edge faster. Use scissors or an inexpensive knife that you have set aside for that purpose.

The following is a list of some of the items I consider necessary in a well-equipped kitchen:

> 3 wooden spoons: a large one with a long handle and two smaller.
> 1 stainless steel set of skimmer, slotted spoon, ladle, large fork, and spatula.
> 1 vegetable peeler.

1 rotary beater and 2 wire whisks.

1 kettle for boiling water quickly.

1 set of stainless steel bowls of graduated sizes. They take up little space and do not chip or crack.

1 white synthetic slab for chopping and slicing. Unlike wood, it will not retain the odors of garlic and onion, and it is easy to clean.

1 coffee maker, preferably the drip type.

1 food processor, if you wish to spend a couple of hundred dollars. First make up your mind to learn how to use it; find out what it will do and what it will not do, and don't treat it as a status symbol.

SETTING THE TABLE

I am highly suspicious of the elaborately cluttered dining table. When I see a table like this, I fear—and many times my fears have been justified—there has been too much emphasis on the setting and little or none on the menu. The table should be a comfortable, harmonious background for the enjoyment of good food and conversation. One case in particular comes to mind: a table set for twelve with four four-branch silver candelabra and an epergne laden with fruit and flowers that obscured guests on the other side of the table as effectively as a well-manicured yew hedge. There were forty-eight small pieces of silver, none of them functional, as well as silver-gilt salts for each guest, elaborate silver frames holding the menu, and five glasses at each place. The overall effect was mind-boggling. The menu was carelessly planned; course after course was presented, each in a heavy cream sauce, with no relief in sight. A fresh green salad would have been as welcome as a pitcher of cool spring water to a traveler in a Sahara caravan. A redeeming feature were the wines: rare, wonderful, and plentiful.

Nevertheless, I am no admirer of the bare "board." A table should be attractive and functional, with ample space for comfortable chairs. The shape of the table is important. If you have any say in the matter and have the space for it, choose a round one rather than an oblong. It is more conducive to conversation and cuts down on formality.

A basic rule for table settings is "high candles and low flowers," if the latter is your centerpiece. More often than not, a piece of decorative porcelain will serve the purpose better. If the table top must be covered, a well-starched white cloth is the perfect background for silver and simple uncut glass. It creates the perfect frame for food, which is, after all, the main feature of the table setting.

The placing of knives, forks, and spoons should be logical. The principle I follow is to place the first utensil used furthest from the plate and work inward following the order of the courses. If the menu is made up of soup, fish, entrée, and dessert, the soup spoon should be on the right-hand side of the place setting furthest from the plate. Working toward the plate on the right side, the fish knife comes next, followed by the entrée knife and the dessert spoon. On the left side of the place setting furthest from the plate is the fish fork. Working toward the plate, the entrée fork comes next, followed by the dessert fork. Coffee spoons should be placed not on the table but with the cups, sugar, and cream on a separate tray. At the turn of the century, when lengthy menus were popular, a table set up by this method left no reason for confusion, no matter how many courses. Remember, work from the outside toward the plate.

Do not be too Spartan when setting up the table, but always bear in mind that comfort takes precedence over decoration.

↓↓↓

THE MENUS

↓↓↓

⇟ ⇟ ⇟

THE MENU

Zucchini Rapées with Sauce Tartare
Salmon en Papillote
Steamed Potatoes
Uncooked Almond Pudding

Since this is the first menu in the book, it was on the tip of my pen to give it the honor of being my favorite, which would have led you to believe, erroneously, that some of the others are not held in such high regard. Fortunately, each menu I've chosen is a favorite, simple to prepare and delicious to eat.

Raw vegetables and a sauce make a splendid first course, followed by fresh salmon, and its partner, the steamed potato, which counteracts the richness of the fish. Lastly, the uncooked almond pudding, a luscious dessert much favored by Edwardians at the turn of the century. The pudding was the specialty of my one-time housekeeper in London, where we referred to it as "Eliza Fury's Uncooked Essex Almond Pudding" (Essex, because that was where she hailed from).

One eight-ounce salmon steak is more than enough for an entrée, and halved it makes an adequate first course, to be followed by a simple entrée. An additional advantage to this recipe is its simple and unmessy method.

THE INGREDIENTS

What You Will Need:

8 to 10 small potatoes
6 small zucchini
2 medium tomatoes
4 large mushroom caps
Lettuce leaves
2 bunches parsley sprigs
2 to 3 shallots
2 lemons
½ dozen large eggs
½ pound unsalted butter

1 pint heavy cream
Sour pickles
Capers
6 8-ounce salmon steaks
½ pound almonds
1 package ladyfingers
Crystallized violets
3 sheets (15 by 18 inches) parchment
  paper

Staples to Have on Hand:

  salt, pepper, vegetable oil, Dijon mustard, flour, granulated sugar, dry white
wine

⇊ ⇊ ⇊

THE WORK SCHEDULE

3 Days Before Serving
1. Check the staples on hand and make your shopping list.
2. Buy everything you will need with the exception of the mushrooms and the salmon.

2 Days Before Serving
1. Order the salmon.
2. Prepare the Sauce Tartare (see page 279), pour it into a screw-top jar, and refrigerate.
3. Prepare, cover, and refrigerate the Almond Pudding (through step 4 of the recipe).

1 Day Before Serving
1. Pick up the salmon and buy the mushrooms.
2. Prepare the sauce for the salmon (through step 3 of the recipe).
3. In the evening, wrap the salmon in the envelopes, brush with melted butter, and refrigerate (through step 5 of the recipe).
4. Peel and shape the potatoes. Put in a bowl and cover with equal parts of milk and water to prevent discoloration. Cover and refrigerate.
5. Set the table and select the wine.

Serving Day
1. *Two hours before serving,* unmold the Almond Pudding and decorate it with whipped cream rosettes and crystallized violets. Refrigerate the pudding on its serving dish until needed.
2. *One hour before serving,* grate the zucchini, cover and refrigerate until needed.
3. Prepare the coffee maker and uncork the wine.
4. *One half-hour before serving,* drain the potatoes, put them in the steamer, and cook for 20 minutes. Keep hot until ready to serve.
5. *One half-hour before serving,* preheat the oven to 400°F. for the papillotes. Brush the packages with the beaten egg and water, and bake for 15 minutes.
6. *Five minutes before serving,* fold the Sauce Tartare into the grated zucchini, arrange on lettuce leaves, and garnish with parsley.

ZUCCHINI RAPÉES

6 small zucchini
Sauce Tartare (see page 279)

Lettuce leaves
Finely chopped parsley

1. Grate the zucchini into a bowl, using the coarsest side of the grater. Cover the bowl with plastic wrap to seal and refrigerate.

2. Just before serving, fold the Sauce Tartare into the zucchini. Arrange on lettuce leaves and sprinkle with finely chopped parsley.

⇓ ⇓ ⇓

SALMON EN PAPILLOTE

2 medium tomatoes
4 large mushroom caps
3 tablespoons unsalted butter
1 tablespoon finely chopped shallots
1 heaping tablespoon flour
⅓ cup dry white wine
1 cup heavy cream
¼ cup finely chopped parsley

6 salmon steaks, 8 ounces each
1 teaspoon salt
¼ teaspoon pepper
3 sheets parchment paper (15 by 18 inches each)
1 egg
1 tablespoon water

1. Plunge the tomatoes into boiling water for 10 seconds. Lift them out, and when cool enough to handle, remove their skins. Cut them in half, remove the seeds, and dice.

2. Wipe the mushroom caps clean with a damp cloth and slice them. Melt the butter in a saucepan, add the tomatoes and mushrooms, and sauté until soft. Add the shallots and cook another 2 minutes.

3. Sprinkle the flour over the vegetables and cook for an additional 2 minutes. Add the wine and continue cooking for 3 or 4 minutes. Pour in the cream and cook, stirring, until the sauce thickens. Remove from the heat and add the parsley.

4. Season the salmon steaks with salt and pepper. Cut each sheet of parchment paper in half and brush each piece with melted butter.

5. Fold each piece in half, then open it and place 2 tablespoons of sauce near the fold. Place a salmon steak on top and cover the steak with 3 tablespoons of sauce. Fold the paper over and pinch the edges to form a half-moon shape. Brush the entire package with melted butter.

6. Preheat the oven to 400°F.

7. Beat the egg with the water and brush the edges of the paper with the egg mixture to seal. Repeat the procedure for the remaining steaks.

8. Place the packaged salmon steaks on a greased baking sheet on the top rack in the oven and bake for 15 minutes. Serve in the paper bags. Cut your own bag first so that your guests, should they be confused, can follow suit.

⇂ ⇂ ⇂

STEAMED POTATOES

8 to 10 small potatoes
Salt

1. Peel and quarter the potatoes. Shape them to look like olives, if you wish, but in any case make them as uniform in size as possible.

2. Put the potatoes in a colander over a pan of boiling water, sprinkle with salt, and cover with a lid to fit. The lid will keep most of the steam in. Steam until tender, about 20 minutes, depending on the size of the potatoes.

3. To keep them hot, remove the lid from the colander and cover the potatoes with a clean kitchen towel.

⇂ ⇂ ⇂

UNCOOKED ALMOND PUDDING

1 package ladyfingers
1 stick (4 ounces) unsalted butter,
   slightly softened
½ cup granulated sugar

3 eggs
1 cup ground almonds
½ cup heavy cream
Crystallized violets for decoration

1. Line a plain 1-quart mold or mixing bowl with dampened cheesecloth. Line the bottom and sides of the mold with the ladyfingers.

2. Beat the butter with the sugar until light and creamy. Add the eggs one at a time, beating well after each addition. Stir in the ground almonds.

3. Pour the mixture into the prepared mold. Cover the top of the pudding with the remaining ladyfingers.

4. Put a saucer or plate with a heavy weight on top of the pudding and refrigerate for 24 hours.

5. Turn the pudding out of the mold and peel off the cheesecloth.

6. Beat the cream until stiff. Decorate the pudding with rosettes of whipped cream and crystallized violets.

⅄⅄⅄

THE MENU

Chicken Mousse
Sole Eventail
Simple Green Salad
Brown Bread Ice Cream

As with the other savory mousses in this book, I recommend serving small portions of the Chicken Mousse. The way I guarantee that my advice will be followed is to make the mousse in half-cup ramekins. On such occasions I would dearly like to revive the custom of the porcelain menu. One could then pace oneself so that he would not overeat one course and leave no room for the next. (A damp cloth removed the writing on the porcelain menu card, leaving it ready for the next day or occasion.)

Sole Eventail is hearty fare, and I serve only a tossed green salad with it.

Brown Bread Ice Cream was the specialty of Gunter's, London's most respected luncheon restaurant, coffeehouse, tea shop, and caterer. The Royal Family were among the clients. I've always thought Brown Bread Ice Cream was England's answer to Italy's Tortoni; there is a definite family resemblance. The title is not likely to seduce you, but please try it and be prepared for a surprise.

THE INGREDIENTS

What You Will Need:

¼ pound mushrooms
2 celery stalks
2 to 3 shallots
1 small onion
1 head Boston lettuce
1 head romaine lettuce
2 lemons
1½ pounds boneless cooked chicken
10 fillets of sole
2 large eggs

Milk
1½ pints heavy cream
¼ pound unsalted butter
2 ounces Gruyère or Parmesan
   cheese
1 cup bread crumbs
1 cup whole wheat bread crumbs
2 envelopes unflavored gelatin
2 tablespoons sunflower seeds

Staples to Have on Hand:

   salt, pepper, ground nutmeg, red wine vinegar, olive oil, vegetable oil, Dijon
mustard, flour, granulated sugar, chicken stock, dry vermouth, dry Madeira,
vanilla extract

THE WORK SCHEDULE

3 Days Before Serving

1. Check the staples on hand and make your shopping list.
2. Buy everything you will need with the exception of the mushrooms and the fish.
3. Prepare the Brown Bread Ice Cream. (It will keep almost indefinitely, so why not double the recipe?)
4. Cook the chicken in salted water just to cover. Let it cool in the cooking liquid, cover, and refrigerate.

2 Days Before Serving

1. Make the Chicken Mousse, wrap securely, and refrigerate.

1 Day Before Serving

1. Buy the mushrooms and the fish. Refrigerate until evening, when the fish can be assembled (through step 2 of the recipe) and refrigerated, covered, until Serving Day.
2. Make the Vinaigrette Dressing (see page 282), pour it into a screw-top jar, and refrigerate.
3. Set the table and select the wine.

Serving Day

1. *Five hours before serving*, or in the morning, unmold the Chicken Mousse onto a suitable platter and refrigerate until serving time.
2. *Two hours before baking*, take the fish out of the refrigerator to allow it to come to room temperature. Make the Mornay Sauce (see page 278).
3. Prepare the salad greens ready for tossing and refrigerate.
4. Prepare the coffee maker and uncork the wine.
5. *One half-hour before serving*, preheat the oven to 375°F., bake the fish for 20 minutes, and complete step 4 of the recipe.
6. Serve the Brown Bread Ice Cream straight from the freezer.

CHICKEN MOUSSE

1 tablespoon unsalted butter
3 tablespoons finely chopped shallots
2 cups chicken stock (see page 276)
2 envelopes unflavored gelatin softened in ¼ cup dry vermouth

2⅓ cups minced cooked chicken
Salt, pepper, and ground nutmeg
3 tablespoons dry Madeira
2 tablespoons lemon juice
Grated peel of 1 lemon
¾ cup cold heavy cream

1. Melt the butter and cook the shallots slowly until soft, taking care that they do not brown; otherwise, the flavor of the mousse will be altered. Add the chicken stock and the gelatin mixture. Blend until smooth. Add the chicken, half at a time (I find the blender produces a very fine purée).

2. Empty the purée into a clean bowl to cool. Season with salt, pepper, and nutmeg to taste. (Add more seasoning than you would think necessary; the cream will tone it down.) Stir in the Madeira and the lemon juice and peel. Refrigerate.

3. When the chicken mixture is almost set, whip the cream until soft peaks form. Fold the cream into the setting chicken mixture. Correct the seasonings and spoon into an oiled 6-cup mold or individual ½-cup ramekins.

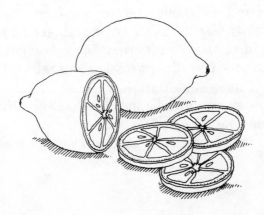

SOLE EVENTAIL

2 celery stalks, chopped very fine
1 small onion, chopped very fine
7 tablespoons unsalted butter
¼ pound mushrooms, chopped very
  fine

Salt and pepper
1 cup bread crumbs
10 fillets of sole
Mornay Sauce (see page 278)
Ground nutmeg

1. Sauté the onion and celery in 4 tablespoons butter until soft. Add the mushrooms and continue cooking for 5 minutes. Add salt and pepper to taste and stir in the bread crumbs. Add more butter to moisten, if necessary.

2. Wipe each piece of fish with a damp cloth. Put a generous spoonful of the sautéed mixture on each piece of fish and fold head to tail. Dot with the remaining butter. Season again with salt and pepper.

3. Preheat the oven to 375°F.

4. Bake for 20 minutes. Season the Mornay Sauce with the nutmeg and mask the fish with the sauce. Glaze under the broiler.

⚡⚡⚡

SIMPLE GREEN SALAD

1 head Boston lettuce
1 head romaine lettuce

Vinaigrette Dressing (see page 282)
2 tablespoons sunflower seeds

Wash and dry the lettuce leaves. Tear them into bite-sized pieces. Toss with just enough Vinaigrette Dressing to coat them, and sprinkle with the sunflower seeds. Toss again.

⚡⚡⚡

BROWN BREAD ICE CREAM

6 ounces whole wheat bread crumbs
2 cups heavy cream
1 cup granulated sugar

½ teaspoon vanilla extract
2 tablespoons water
2 egg whites

1. Dry the bread crumbs in the oven until they are lightly browned and crisp.

2. Beat the cream until stiff, adding ¾ cup sugar gradually. Beat in the vanilla extract.

3. Simmer the remaining sugar and water together for 2 or 3 minutes. Stir into the bread crumbs and fold the mixture into the beaten cream.

4. Beat the egg whites until they hold peaks, and fold gently into the cream and crumb mixture.

5. Freeze in a 9 × 5-inch loaf pan (you can coat the inside of the pan with melted chocolate, if you wish) or in individual ramekins. Unmold onto a cold serving platter or cold dishes to serve.

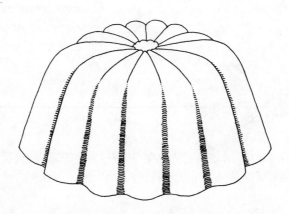

⅍ ⅍ ⅍

THE MENU

Oxtail Soup
Petits Turbans of Sole
Simple Green Salad (see page 33)
Chocolate Truffles

Most people take for granted that Oxtail Soup is rich and heavy. On the contrary, it is a clear, light aromatic liquid. Preceding a rich fish dish, it acts as a stimulant to the appetite and starts the gastric juices flowing. It keeps well frozen and can be a useful first course to call on for impromptu parties.

The Petits Turbans of Sole is beautiful both in appearance and in taste. With the use of a food processor, its preparation is a simple matter compared with the days when a pestle and mortar and a hair sieve were the only kitchen appliances available. A green salad is an appropriate accompaniment.

Chocolate Truffles with coffee will satisfy those with a sweet tooth.

THE INGREDIENTS

What You Will Need:

3 celery stalks
1 carrot
1 small turnip
1 onion
2 lemons
1 bunch parsley sprigs
1 head Boston lettuce
1 head romaine lettuce

2 to 2½ pounds oxtail, cut into pieces
3 whole sole, filleted
10 ounces small shrimp
¾ pound unsalted butter
½ dozen large eggs
1 pint heavy cream
1 pound semisweet chocolate
2 tablespoons sunflower seeds

Staples to Have on Hand:

salt, pepper, peppercorns, whole cloves, ground nutmeg, dried thyme, bay leaf, red wine vinegar, olive oil, vegetable oil, Dijon mustard, flour, granulated sugar, cocoa powder, confectioner's sugar, tomato purée, port wine, dry white wine, dark rum

THE WORK SCHEDULE

3 Days Before Serving

1. Check the staples on hand and make your shopping list.
2. Buy everything you will need with the exception of the fish and the shrimp.

2 Days Before Serving

1. Buy the fish and the shrimp.
2. Prepare the Oxtail Soup (through step 2 of the recipe). Allow at least 4 hours for cooking. Remove the vegetables and discard. Reserve the meat; wrap and refrigerate. Cool the broth, then cover and refrigerate.
3. Make the Chocolate Truffles. Store in an airtight container in the refrigerator.

1 Day Before Serving

1. Prepare the Petits Turbans (through step 4 of the recipe).
2. Make the Vinaigrette Dressing (see page 282), put it into a screw-top jar, and refrigerate.
3. Set the table and select the wine.

Serving Day

1. *One hour before serving,* remove the broth and the meat from the refrigerator. Discard any fat on the broth and the meat.
2. *One hour before serving,* remove the fish from the refrigerator and preheat the oven to 350°F. Cover baking dish with buttered wax paper (see step 5 of recipe) and bake for 30 minutes.
3. Prepare sauce and complete recipe (steps 6 through 8).
4. Arrange the truffles on a suitable dish.
5. Prepare the salad greens ready for tossing and refrigerate.
6. Prepare the coffee maker and uncork the wine.
7. *Ten minutes before serving,* reheat the soup and complete step 3 of the recipe.

↯ ↯ ↯

OXTAIL SOUP

4 tablespoons unsalted butter

1 large oxtail, 2 to 2½ pounds, cut into pieces

3 celery stalks, chopped

1 carrot, sliced

1 small turnip, peeled and sliced

8 to 10 peppercorns

1 onion, studded with 4 whole cloves

Bouquet garni (parsley stalks, pinch of dried thyme, small bay leaf) tied in a cheesecloth bag

2 quarts water

Salt and pepper

¼ cup port wine

1. Melt 1 or 2 tablespoons of butter in a heavy skillet and brown the oxtail, celery, carrot, and turnip. Add more butter as needed.

2. Transfer to a stockpot and add the peppercorns, studded onion, bouquet garni, and water. Bring to a boil, cover, and simmer for 4 hours, or until the meat falls off the bones. Strain the soup into a clean bowl and discard the vegetables. Remove the fat from the meat and put the meat in a bowl. Cool both the broth and the meat, cover, and refrigerate until needed.

3. When ready to serve, put the meat and the broth into a saucepan and season with salt and pepper to taste. Reheat and add the port wine just before serving.

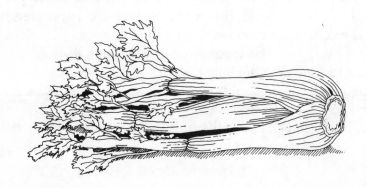

PETITS TURBANS OF SOLE

THE FISH:
3 whole sole, filleted
10 ounces small shrimp
2 egg whites
1 cup heavy cream
1 tablespoon tomato purée
½ teaspoon ground nutmeg
Grated peel of 1 lemon
Salt and pepper
Unsalted butter

½ cup dry white wine
½ cup parsley sprigs, chopped

THE SAUCE:
2 tablespoons unsalted butter
2 tablespoons flour
2 cups liquid from cooking fish
½ cup heavy cream
Salt, pepper, and lemon juice

1. Cut each fillet in half and remove the connecting thread. There will now be 12 strips of fish.

2. Shell, devein, and wash the shrimp. There should be approximately 8 ounces of shrimp after cleaning.

3. Put the shrimp and the egg whites in a food processor and purée. Add the cream, tomato purée, nutmeg, lemon peel, and salt and pepper to taste and blend for 30 seconds. Bring a little water to a simmer and poach a tablespoon of the fish purée for a minute or so. Taste for seasoning and add what is needed to the mixture.

4. Lightly butter a 10×7×2-inch ovenproof dish. Roll strips of the sole loosely so as to leave a hole for the fish purée. Arrange the rolls in the dish so that they do not touch. Fill the holes with the purée and pour the wine into the dish. Cover and refrigerate until needed.

5. Preheat the oven to 350°F. Cover the baking dish with a piece of buttered wax paper, buttered side down. Bake in the middle of the oven for 30 minutes.

6. Drain the liquid from the dish into a measuring cup and keep the fish warm. The liquid should measure 2 cups.

(Continued)

7. Melt 2 tablespoons of butter in a small heavy saucepan. Add the flour and stir and cook for 1 or 2 minutes. Do not allow the roux to brown. Remove the pan from the heat and pour in the liquid from the fish. Stir until smooth. Add the cream and return to the heat, cooking slowly until the sauce is as thick as heavy cream. Season with salt, pepper, and lemon juice to taste.

8. To serve, pour a little sauce over the fish and sprinkle the sauced fish with the chopped parsley. Serve the remaining sauce warm in a sauceboat.

CHOCOLATE TRUFFLES

1 pound semisweet chocolate	6 tablespoons dark rum
½ pound unsalted butter, softened	¾ cup cocoa powder
6 egg yolks	¾ cup confectioner's sugar

Melt the chocolate over simmering water. Beat in the butter, egg yolks, and rum with a whisk until the mixture is workable and can be shaped into round balls 1 inch in diameter. Roll the truffles in cocoa and confectioner's sugar. Put into an airtight container and refrigerate. Makes 80 to 90 pieces.

⇟ ⇟ ⇟

THE MENU

Panache
Poached Salmon with Sauce Verte
Cucumber Salad
Lemon Curd and Whole Wheat Toast

Panache, if I remember rightly, originated in Majorca, where the cook would sit and rub all the vegetables—with the exception of diced green pepper—through a fine hair sieve. Thanks to food processors, we are spared that laborious and time-consuming chore.

Lemon Curd keeps well when refrigerated. I do not believe in using cornstarch in its preparation. Fresh eggs, unsalted butter, sugar, and lemon juice are the principal ingredients. Use coarse whole wheat bread for the toast.

Until quite recently, fish on the whole was badly cooked, principally for lack of knowledge. Hot fish—poached, baked, or broiled—should be served right after it's been cooked. A cold poached fish is allowed to cool in the poaching liquid. If poached fish is to be served hot, it is allowed to rest in the liquid for 10 minutes or so. Letting the fish rest or cool in its own liquid will assure greater retention of moisture.

The Fisheries Association of British Columbia has put together a foolproof method for cooking fish. Measure the fish, it says, through its thickest part and cook it for 10 minutes for every inch of its thickness. To bake, preheat the oven and bake for 10 minutes per inch of thickness at 450°F. Use the same method for poaching. Bring the court bouillon to a boil, add the fish, and apply the same technique for timing the fish when the liquid boils for the second time. Madame Prunier, one of the greatest exponents of fish cooking, described poaching as "simmering in a trembling court bouillon, so that cooking proceeds by gradual penetration of heat into the fish."

THE INGREDIENTS

What You Will Need:

1 large Spanish onion
1 green pepper
10 ounces green beans
2 celery stalks
2 carrots
1 yellow onion
1 bunch watercress
3 large bunches parsley sprigs
2 small bunches tarragon
1 European cucumber or 2 domestic
   cucumbers
1 bunch fresh dill

6 lemons
1 8- to 10-pound whole salmon,
   cleaned
1 dozen large eggs
½ pint sour cream
¼ pound unsalted butter
2 4-ounce bottles artichoke hearts
Stuffed olives
Pimiento
Whole wheat bread
Dry white wine

Staples to Have on Hand:

   salt, pepper, peppercorns, bay leaf, olive oil, red wine vinegar, Dijon
mustard, granulated sugar

THE WORK SCHEDULE

3 Days Before Serving

1. Check the staples on hand and make your shopping list.
2. Buy everything you will need with the exception of the fresh herbs, watercress, salmon, and whole wheat bread.

2 Days Before Serving

1. Order the salmon and buy the herbs, watercress, and whole wheat bread.
2. Prepare the Lemon Curd and store in the refrigerator in a screw-top jar. It will keep safely for 2 weeks.
3. Make the mayonnaise (see page 280) and Sauce Verte (see page 280) and cover and refrigerate.

1 Day Before Serving

1. Pick up the salmon. Prepare the court bouillon.
2. Late in the day, poach the fish in the court bouillon, cool, cover, and refrigerate.
3. Prepare the cucumber for the salad (through step 1 of the recipe). Cover and refrigerate.
4. Prepare the Panache (through step 5 of the recipe) but do not garnish. Cover and refrigerate.
5. Set the table and select the wine.

Serving Day

1. *Two hours before serving,* remove the Panache from the refrigerator and garnish. Serve it at room temperature.
2. *Two hours before serving,* remove the salmon from the court bouillon and arrange it on a platter. Serve at room temperature with the Sauce Verte.
3. Prepare the sauce for the cucumber (step 2 of the recipe). Mix the drained cucumber with the sauce and spoon onto a serving platter or into a salad bowl.
4. Slice the whole wheat bread in readiness for toasting.
5. Spoon the Lemon Curd into a suitable serving dish.
6. Prepare the coffee maker and uncork the wine.

PANACHE

1 large Spanish onion	4 eggs
½ cup olive oil	1 teaspoon salt
1 green pepper	¼ teaspoon pepper
10 ounces (approximately) green beans, lightly cooked	Several sliced stuffed green olives for garnish
2 4-ounce bottles of artichoke hearts, drained	1 pimiento, cut into strips, for garnish

1. Slice the onion thinly and cook it in the olive oil until it is transparent; do not allow the onion to brown.

2. Slice and dice the green pepper. Cook the beans in fast-boiling water for 5 minutes.

3. Put the beans, artichoke hearts, onion, and oil into a blender or food processor and purée. Beat the eggs to a froth and mix them with the puréed vegetables and diced green pepper. Season with salt and pepper.

4. Preheat the oven to 350°F.

5. Transfer the vegetable mixture to a well-buttered 7 × 10 × 2-inch oven-proof dish, preferably earthenware. Bake for 50 minutes. Cool, cover, and refrigerate.

6. At serving time, garnish with the olives and pimiento. Serve at room temperature.

POACHED SALMON

2 celery stalks, roughly chopped
2 carrots, washed and sliced
1 onion, peeled and sliced
6 to 8 parsley stalks
1 small bay leaf
8 peppercorns

4 quarts water
2 tablespoons salt
2 cups dry white wine
1 8- to 10-pound salmon, cleaned
Sauce Verte (see page 280)

1. Put the celery, carrots, onion, parsley, bay leaf, and peppercorns in a cheesecloth bag and add to the water, salt, and wine in a pan large enough to hold the fish. Bring to a boil, reduce the heat, and simmer, covered, for 30 to 40 minutes.

2. Discard the bag of aromatics and bring the court bouillon to a boil once again.

3. Measure the thickness of the fish, add to the boiling court bouillon, reduce the heat, and simmer in a trembling court bouillon for 10 minutes for each inch of thickness of the fish. Remove from the heat 5 minutes before the allotted time to allow the fish to cool in the court bouillon. When cool, cover and refrigerate. Serve with Sauce Verte.

⇊ ⇊ ⇊

CUCUMBER SALAD

1 large European cucumber or 2 domestic cucumbers
1 cup sour cream
½ cup mayonnaise (see page 280)

Lemon juice, salt, and pepper
2 tablespoons snipped dill (dill is too delicate to be chopped)

1. Remove strips of skin from the cucumber. (It can be tough.) Slice or cube the cucumber, put it in a bowl, cover, and refrigerate.

2. Combine the sour cream and mayonnaise in a bowl. Mix thoroughly and season with lemon juice, salt, and pepper to taste. Stir in the dill and mix again. Cover and refrigerate until needed.

3. To serve, drain the cucumber and stir it into the sauce.

LEMON CURD

1 stick (4 ounces) unsalted butter   Juice of 4 lemons
½ cup granulated sugar   Grated peel of 3 lemons
4 egg yolks   Whole wheat toast
1 egg

1. Melt the butter and dissolve the sugar in the top of a double boiler over gently simmering water.

2. Blend the egg yolks and egg thoroughly. Add the eggs, lemon juice, and grated lemon peel to the sugar and butter and cook, stirring now and again, until heavy and thick.

3. Cool and store in screw-top jars. It will keep for two weeks in the refrigerator.

4. To serve, spread the Lemon Curd on the toast.

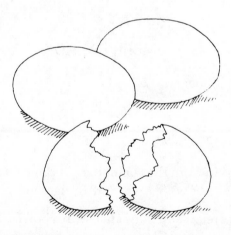

↯ ↯ ↯

THE MENU

Tomato Ice
Stuffed Striped Bass
Steamed Potatoes (see page 27)
Treacle Tart

Tomato Ice puts me on the horns of a dilemma. Should it be served as a first course or a last—appetizer or dessert? Is it a fruit or a vegetable? It could be either, and in this menu it comes first. It is a stimulant that does wonders for the palate.

Bass needs no introduction. It is a superb fish when cooked with loving care. It may be served hot, at room temperature, or cold. All that is needed to dress it up is a few steamed potatoes if it is to be served hot or at room temperature, or a tossed fresh green salad if it is to be served cold.

Treacle Tart is English and is not well known in this country. Treacle, or Golden Syrup, which is not unlike molasses, can be found in specialty food shops.

THE INGREDIENTS

What You Will Need:

4 lemons

1 bunch parsley sprigs

1 bunch chives

½ pound shallots

8 to 10 small potatoes

5- to 6-pound striped bass, cleaned

1 dozen large eggs

½ pound unsalted butter

½ cup heavy cream

1 cup Italian plum tomatoes

½ cup bread crumbs

1 cup Golden Syrup (treacle)

Dry white wine

Staples to Have on Hand:

   salt, pepper, dried dill, vegetable oil, vegetable shortening, granulated sugar, flour

THE WORK SCHEDULE

2 Days Before Serving
1. Check the staples on hand and make your shopping list.
2. Buy everything you will need with the exception of the fish. Treacle is sold under the name of Golden Syrup and is made in England.

1 Day Before Serving
1. Buy the fish and refrigerate until Serving Day.
2. Make the pastry for the Treacle Tart. Allow the pastry to rest, then bake the shell, ready for filling and completing the following day.
3. Prepare the ingredients for the Tomato Ice (through step 1 of the recipe), ready for freezing on Serving Day. Refrigerate; if frozen too soon, you may find it difficult to break the ice down.
4. Peel the potatoes, put them in a bowl, and cover them with half milk and half water to prevent them from darkening. Cover and refrigerate.
5. Set the table and select the wine.

Serving Day
1. Complete the Treacle Tart. Do not refrigerate.
2. *Four or five hours before serving,* begin freezing the Tomato Ice. Keep an eye on it to make sure it does not freeze solid. Put the serving glasses or plates in the refrigerator to chill.
3. *One hour before serving,* scramble the eggs for the fish filling. Stuff and bake the fish.
4. *One half-hour before serving,* drain the potatoes and put them in the steamer.
5. Prepare the coffee maker and uncork the wine.

⅄ ⅄ ⅄

TOMATO ICE

½ cup granulated sugar
¼ cup hot water
1 cup Italian plum tomatoes, sieved

Juice of 1 lemon, approximately 3
tablespoons, or to taste
Lemon wedges for garnish

1. Dissolve the sugar in hot water. Bring to a boil and simmer for exactly 2 minutes. The temperature on a candy thermometer will be 212°F. Cool, stir in sieved tomatoes and lemon juice, cover, and refrigerate.

2. Transfer the ice mixture to a freezer tray and freeze, stirring from time to time to mix. The Tomato Ice is ready when it resembles wet snow. Serve in small glasses, garnished with a wedge of lemon.

⇟⇟⇟

STUFFED STRIPED BASS

1 striped bass, 5 to 6 pounds, cleaned
5 eggs
Salt
Pepper
1 tablespoon finely chopped parlsey
½ tablespoon finely chopped chives

¼ teaspoon dried dill
2 tablespoons unsalted butter
1 cup chopped shallots or scallions
2 cups dry white wine
3 egg yolks
½ cup heavy cream

1. Preheat the oven to 425°F.

2. Wash the cleaned bass under cold running water; drain and pat dry.

3. Break the eggs into a mixing bowl and beat them. Add ½ teaspoon salt, ¼ teaspoon pepper, the parsley, chives, and dill. Mix well.

4. Melt the butter in a heavy skillet. Pour in the egg mixture and stir with a fork over low heat until the eggs are cooked but not dry. Stuff the bass with the egg mixture and sew up the opening.

5. Oil a baking dish and make a bed of the shallots. Pour the wine over and put the bass on top. Dust lightly with salt and pepper. Bake for 25 to 30 minutes, basting frequently with the pan juices.

6. Remove the bass to a heated serving platter and keep it warm. Strain the pan juices into a saucepan and discard the solids.

7. Beat the egg yolks and stir in the cream. Combine the mixture gradually with the pan juices. Heat, stirring, over low heat until the sauce thickens. Be careful that the sauce does not boil. Serve the sauce in a warm sauceboat.

⅄ ⅄ ⅄

TREACLE TART

1 cup Golden Syrup (treacle)
½ cup white bread crumbs
Grated peel of 1 lemon

1 prepared 9-inch shell of Short Pastry (see following recipe)

1. Preheat the oven to 425°F.

2. In a bowl mix the syrup, bread crumbs, and peel together. Pour into the prepared shell.

3. Bake the tart for 20 to 30 minutes. The top should be a rich golden brown all over. Serve at room temperature.

⅄ ⅄ ⅄

SHORT PASTRY

2 cups flour
½ teaspoon salt
1 stick (4 ounces) unsalted butter

3 tablespoons vegetable shortening
2½ to 3 tablespoons cold water
1 egg beaten with 1 tablespoon water

1. Blend the flour, salt, butter, and shortening together with a pastry blender or two knives. Gradually add the cold water, as little as possible, but sufficient to bind the pastry.

2. On a pastry board or cloth, smear with the heel of your hand, starting from the outside, and pressing hard. Form the pastry into a ball, wrap, and allow it to rest for about 2 hours before rolling out.

3. Preheat the oven to 400°F.

4. Roll the pastry ⅛ inch thick. Line a 9-inch pie dish with the dough. Trim the pastry and prick it all over with a fork. Bake for 10 to 15 minutes.

5. Brush the partially baked shell with the beaten egg and water. Reduce the oven temperature to 350°F., and bake the shell for 10 minutes longer. Cool.

↯ ↯ ↯

THE MENU

Cucumber Mousse
Madras Shrimp
Orzo
Dolce Maddalena

There are many times when I am tempted to serve the Cucumber Mousse with Madras Shrimp and forget about the mousse as a course by itself. Cucumbers, cool and sharp, marry well with almost any curried dish, and Madras Shrimp is no exception. It's an idea—try it sometime.

Curried dishes call for a starchy accompaniment in one form or another. Rice and pasta are the most obvious choices, but in my opinion orzo is the most suitable starch to serve with this dish. Greek in origin, orzo is a pasta made in the shape of rice. It reheats successfully.

Wine should never be served with curry. Beer or lager goes best with this spicy dish.

Many years ago on my way to Corfu, I stayed for one night at a beach resort outside Rimini. It was late autumn, and the only accommodation to be had was above a small café. We dined off pasta and a well-grilled fish and for dessert were offered Dolce Maddalena, the house specialty. It was so good, I asked for the recipe, quite expecting a curt refusal. To my complete astonishment, however, I was cordially given three or four copies of the recipe from a Xeroxed pile. So much for a closely guarded secret! When I got back to New York, I promptly added it to my collection of recipes that could be prepared in June and served in January.

THE INGREDIENTS

What You Will Need:

3 cucumbers
1 bunch parsley sprigs
2 lemons
2 large onions
1 large green pepper
1 celery stalk
3 pounds shrimp
2 large eggs
½ cup heavy cream
½ pound ricotta

1 pound orzo
1 cup tomato purée
1 pound canned Italian plum tomatoes
1 envelope unflavored gelatin
¼ pound candied fruit
4 ounces bitter chocolate
1 package ladyfingers
16 Amaretti macaroons
Lager or light beer

Staples to Have on Hand:

salt, pepper, cayenne, bay leaves, imported curry powder, garlic clove, red wine vinegar, olive oil, vegetable oil, Dijon mustard, Worcestershire sauce, granulated sugar, sweet Marsala

THE WORK SCHEDULE

3 Days Before Serving

1. Check the staples on hand and make your shopping list.
2. Buy everything you will need with the exception of the shrimp.
3. Prepare the Dolce Maddalena and freeze it.
4. Make the mayonnaise for the mousse (see page 280), cover, and refrigerate.

2 Days Before Serving

1. Prepare the Cucumber Mousse, wrap securely to prevent moisture loss, and refrigerate.
2. Prepare the Madras sauce (through step 2 in the recipe) in readiness for cooking the shrimp. Cool, cover, and refrigerate.

1 Day Before Serving

1. Buy the shrimp. Peel, devein, wash, cover, and refrigerate them.
2. Buy lager or light beer to serve with the shrimp dish.
3. Set the table and select a dessert wine.

Serving Day

1. *One hour before serving*, unmold the Cucumber Mousse onto a suitable platter and garnish. Refrigerate until serving time.
2. *One hour before serving*, unmold the Dolce Maddalena. Refrigerate until serving time to give it time to soften slightly.
3. Heat the sauce for the shrimp in readiness for heating the shrimp.
4. Prepare the coffee maker.
5. Cook the orzo according to package directions and keep it hot in a colander or strainer over a pot of simmering water for no more than ½ hour.
6. Open the beer at the last minute.

CUCUMBER MOUSSE

2 whole cucumbers
1 envelope unflavored gelatin
½ cup mayonnaise (see page 280)
Salt and pepper
1 teaspoon Worcestershire sauce

Juice of 1 lemon
½ cup heavy cream
Parsley sprigs for garnish
Cucumber slices for garnish

1. Peel the cucumbers, cut them in half lengthwise, and remove the seeds. Shred the cucumbers into a mixing bowl.

2. Soften the gelatin in ¼ cup cold water and set aside.

3. Combine the mayonnaise, salt and pepper to taste, Worcestershire sauce, lemon juice, and softened gelatin.

4. Whip the cream until it holds soft peaks and fold into the mayonnaise mixture. Add the cucumber and refrigerate until it begins to set.

5. Spoon the mixture into a chilled 1-quart mold, cover and chill for at least 2 hours.

6. To serve, unmold the mousse and decorate with sprigs of parsley and thin slices of cucumber.

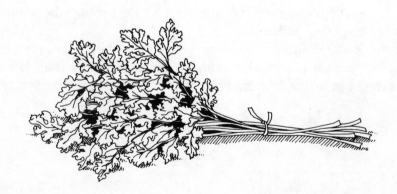

MADRAS SHRIMP

⅓ cup olive oil
2 cups finely chopped onion
1 cup finely chopped green pepper
½ cup finely chopped celery
1 can (16 ounces) Italian plum tomatoes with basil
1 cup tomato purée
¼ teaspoon cayenne

1 clove garlic, peeled and finely chopped
2 medium bay leaves
Salt and pepper
2 tablespoons imported curry powder
3 pounds cooked shrimp

1. Heat the oil in a heavy 2-quart pot. Add the onion, green pepper, and celery and cook until soft, stirring frequently. Add the tomatoes, tomato purée, cayenne, garlic, bay leaves, and salt and pepper to taste.

2. Bring to a boil and add the curry powder. Lower the heat, cover, and simmer for 20 minutes. If the sauce seems too thick, thin it with a little chicken stock or water. Cool, cover, and refrigerate.

3. To serve, add the shrimp to the sauce and simmer for 10 minutes.

⅄ ⅄ ⅄

DOLCE MADDALENA

1 package ladyfingers, or enough to line a 1-quart charlotte mold or bowl
¼ cup sweet Marsala
2 eggs, separated
½ cup granulated sugar

¾ cup ricotta
16 double Amaretti macaroons, crushed
4 ounces bitter chocolate, grated
½ cup candied fruit

1. Sprinkle the ladyfingers with the Marsala. Line the sides and bottom of the mold with the ladyfingers, curved side to the outside.

(Continued)

2. Beat the egg yolks with the sugar until thick and heavy. Mix in the ricotta. Stir in the crushed macaroons, grated chocolate, and candied fruit.

3. Beat the egg whites until they hold stiff peaks. Fold into the ricotta mixture and spoon into the prepared mold. Tap the mold to get rid of any air pockets. Cover the top with more Marsala-soaked ladyfingers. Cover the mold with plastic wrap and freeze.

4. Unmold and serve in thin slivers. It is ravishingly rich. The Dolce Maddalena keeps well frozen.

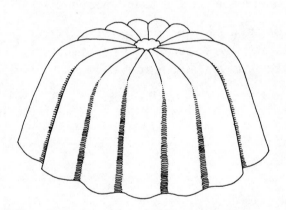

↯↯↯

THE MENU

Spinach Soup
Roulade of Crab
Simple Green Salad (see page 33)
Sabayon Frappé aux Pêches

Spinach Soup, served before the very rich roulade of fish—whether it be white fish, lobster, or crabmeat—prepares the palate and assures an appetite. The roulade is well worth the trouble it takes to make. It is a fine party dish, one that can well be served at room temperature accompanied by a green salad. Make the serving small to allow for a small helping of Sabayon on its own or over fresh peaches. All along it has been my policy not to shun over-rich dishes, but to make the servings small. If I think I have overdone the calories for the day, well and good; I will cut down on what I eat the following day to make up for the excess.

THE INGREDIENTS

What You Will Need:

1 medium onion
1 head Boston lettuce
1 head romaine lettuce
1 orange or 2 lemons
2 ripe peaches
4 10-ounce packages frozen spinach
1 pound crabmeat
1 quart milk

2½ dozen large eggs
½ pound unsalted butter
½ cup heavy cream
4 ounces Parmesan cheese
2 tablespoons anchovy paste
2 tablespoons sunflower seeds
2 sheets (12 by 18 inches) parchment
   paper

Staples to Have on Hand:

   salt, pepper, ground nutmeg, red wine vinegar, olive oil, Dijon mustard, chicken stock (see page 276), flour, granulated sugar, Madeira

THE WORK SCHEDULE

2 Days Before Serving

1. Check the staples on hand and make your shopping list.
2. Buy everything you will need with the exception of the salad greens.
3. Prepare the Sabayon Frappé, cover, and freeze.
4. Make the Vinaigrette Dressing (see page 282) and store it in a screw-top jar in the refrigerator.

1 Day Before Serving

1. Buy the salad greens. Wash and dry them well. Put into plastic bags and refrigerate.
2. Prepare the Spinach Soup (through Step 3 of the recipe). Cover and refrigerate.
3. Prepare the Roulade. Roll it up carefully, cover tightly, and refrigerate.
4. Set the table and select the wine.

Serving Day

1. *Three hours before serving,* take the Roulade out of the refrigerator to allow it to come to room temperature for serving.
2. *One half-hour before serving,* transfer the Sabayon from the freezer to the refrigerator.
3. Arrange the salad ready for tossing at the last minute.
4. *Ten minutes before serving,* heat the Spinach Soup.
5. Prepare the coffee maker and uncork the wine.

SPINACH SOUP

4 10-ounce packages frozen spinach
½ medium onion, chopped
1 tablespoon unsalted butter
4 cups chicken stock (see page 276)

Salt, pepper, and ground nutmeg
Yolk of 1 hard-boiled egg, sieved, for
garnish

1. Defrost the spinach and squeeze out most of the water.

2. Sauté the onion in the butter. Add the spinach and cook over low heat until the spinach is hot. Purée in a blender or food processor with 2 cups of stock.

3. Stir into the remaining stock and season with salt, pepper, and nutmeg to taste. Cover and refrigerate.

4. To serve, reheat slowly just before serving to avoid discoloring. Garnish with the sieved egg yolk.

⇓ ⇓ ⇓

ROULADE OF CRAB

3 cups Béchamel Sauce (see page 278)
Ground nutmeg
2 tablespoons anchovy paste
1 pound crabmeat
8 eggs, separated

⅔ cup lightly packed grated Parmesan cheese
Salt and pepper
16 eggs, hard-boiled and finely
chopped

1. Preheat the oven to 400°F. Line a 12 × 18-inch baking sheet with buttered parchment paper.

2. Season the Béchamel Sauce with nutmeg to taste and the anchovy paste.

3. Combine 1 cup of the sauce with the crabmeat. Beat in the egg yolks and one third of the cheese. Season with salt and pepper to taste.

4. Beat the egg whites until firm but not dry and fold them into the crab mixture with a large metal spoon. Spread the mixture in the prepared baking sheet. Bake on the top shelf of the oven for 10 to 15 minutes, or until well risen and firm to the touch.

5. Have ready a large sheet of parchment paper sprinkled with the remainder of the cheese. Quickly turn the roulade out onto this and strip off the paper on which it was baked.

6. Add the chopped eggs to the remaining sauce and spread the mixture over the roulade. Trim the sides, then tilt the paper and roll up as you would a jelly roll. Cover tightly and refrigerate.

↡ ↡ ↡

SABAYON FRAPPÉ AUX PÊCHES

3 egg yolks
1 egg
½ cup granulated sugar
4 to 8 tablespoons Madeira
½ cup heavy cream, beaten stiff

1 teaspoon grated orange or lemon peel
2 peaches
¼ cup granulated sugar
½ cup water

1. Beat the egg yolks, egg, ½ cup sugar, and Madeira in a large ceramic bowl until well blended. Put the bowl over a pan of simmering water and whisk until frothy and stiff. Remove from the pan, put in cold water, and beat the mixture until it has cooled. Fold in the beaten cream and grated peel.

2. Put the peaches in boiling water for 5 minutes. Remove, peel, and slice them. If the peaches are unripe, put them in a pan with ¼ cup sugar and ½ cup water and simmer slowly for 10 to 15 minutes, or until they are tender. Drain and cool.

3. Put the peach slices on the bottom of a serving dish or individual dishes. Chill. Then pour the Sabayon over the peaches and freeze for at least 1 hour before serving.

↓↓↓

THE MENU

Chick-Pea Salad
Crêpes de Volaille with Mornay Sauce
Ananas Glacés Orange

Many years ago food editor Clementine Paddleford gave me a recipe for Chick-Pea Salad. It is a recipe I never tire of, either on its own as a luncheon dish, or in small portions as part of a three-course menu.

Crêpes or pancakes are items that should be mastered sooner or later by every cook. There is little that can't be used to fill them, and without a filling they are wonderful served hot sprinkled with lemon juice and a fine sugar. They may be cooked ahead of time and frozen (without a filling), provided they are wrapped and securely sealed with a sheet of wax paper between each one. The dessert is all the better for being made a day ahead of time, but don't sprinkle it with the almonds until just before serving or they will become soggy.

THE INGREDIENTS

What You Will Need:

3 scallions
2 tomatoes
1 celery stalk
1 carrot
1 onion
3 parsley sprigs
Salad greens
1 pineapple
4 thin-skinned oranges
1 lemon

3½- to 4-pound chicken
¼ pound hard salami
½ dozen large eggs
¼ pound unsalted butter
1 quart milk
4 ounces Parmesan cheese
½ pound dried chick-peas, or 1
    1-pound can
¼ cup slivered almonds
Pimiento-stuffed olives

Staples to Have on Hand:

   salt, pepper, peppercorns, bay leaf, garlic clove, tarragon vinegar, olive oil, vegetable oil, ground nutmeg, flour, granulated sugar, orange-flavored liqueur, brandy.

⇊⇊⇊

THE WORK SCHEDULE

3 Days Before Serving

1. Check the staples on hand and make your shopping list.
2. Buy everything you will need.
3. If you are using dried chick-peas, put them on to soak overnight.

2 Days Before Serving

1. Poach the chicken. Strain the broth, discarding all the vegetables and seasonings. When cool enough to handle, skin the chicken and remove the meat from the bones. Put the chicken in a bowl and pour enough broth over it to moisten it. Cool, cover, and refrigerate.
2. Prepare the crêpes (steps 3 and 4 of the recipe), store as for freezing (a piece of wax paper between each one and securely wrapped), and refrigerate.
3. Prepare the pineapple and oranges for the dessert, following the directions carefully. Cool, cover, and refrigerate. Reserve the syrup for Serving Day. Cool, cover, and refrigerate.
4. If using dried chick-peas, cook them until tender, but do not drain. Cool, cover, and refrigerate.

1 Day Before Serving

1. Make the Mornay Sauce (see page 278) and fill the crêpes and arrange them in their serving dish. Cover and refrigerate filled crêpes and reserved Mornay Sauce until Serving Day.
2. Arrange the dessert on its serving dish, but do not complete the syrup until Serving Day. (The almonds, as I have indicated earlier, will not be scattered on top until the last minute.)
3. Set the table and select the wine.

Serving Day

1. *Two hours before serving*, take the prepared crêpes, dessert, and chick-peas out of the refrigerator. Drain the chick-peas (step 2 of the recipe).
2. *One half-hour before serving*, complete the dessert by cooking the syrup and spooning it over the fruit with the liqueur. Sprinkle the almonds on at this time.
3. *One half-hour before serving*, toss the salad with the dressing (step 3 of the recipe) and chill.
4. *Fifteen minutes before serving*, preheat the oven to 450°F. for heating the crêpes. Spoon the reserved Mornay Sauce over the crêpes and bake for 10 minutes (step 9 of the recipe).
5. Prepare the coffee maker and uncork the wine.
6. *Just before serving*, complete step 4 of the recipe for chick-pea salad.

CHICK-PEA SALAD

1½ cups dried chick-peas, or 1
   1-pound can cooked chick-peas
½ cup tarragon vinegar
½ cup olive or vegetable oil
1 clove garlic, peeled and crushed
½ teaspoon salt
Pinch of pepper

½ cup sliced pimiento-stuffed olives
¼ pound hard salami, cut in strips
Salad greens
3 tablespoons finely chopped scallions
2 tomatoes, diced

1. If dried peas are used, soak overnight in cold water to cover. Drain and cover with water. Bring to a boil and simmer for 1 hour and 45 minutes, or until tender. Cool, cover, and refrigerate.

2. When ready to assemble the salad, drain, rinse the peas with cold water, and drain again.

3. Combine the vinegar, oil, garlic, salt, and pepper in a bowl. Add the drained chick-peas, olives, and salami. Mix lightly and chill.

4. Line a bowl with the salad greens and spoon in the chick-peas. Sprinkle with the scallions and garnish with the tomatoes.

CRÊPES DE VOLAILLE WITH MORNAY SAUCE

1 3½- to 4-pound chicken
1 celery stalk with leaves
1 carrot, scraped
1 onion, peeled
3 parsley sprigs
1 bay leaf
4 peppercorns
1½ teaspoons salt
1½ cups flour

2½ cups milk
2 tablespoons vegetable oil
2 eggs
2 egg yolks
Oil for cooking
Ground nutmeg
4 cups Mornay Sauce (see page 278)
¾ cup freshly grated Parmesan cheese

1. Put the chicken in a large saucepan with the celery, carrot, onion, parsley, bay leaf, peppercorns, and 1 teaspoon salt. Add water to cover and bring to a boil. Partially cover and simmer for about 1 hour.

2. Remove the chicken from the pot, and, when cool enough to handle, skin it and remove the meat from the bones. Discard the skin and bones and put the chicken pieces in a bowl. Strain the broth over the chicken, cover, and refrigerate.

3. In a bowl combine the flour, ½ teaspoon salt, and ½ cup milk. Add the 2 tablespoons oil while beating. Continue to beat while adding the eggs and egg yolks. Beat the batter until it is smooth and thoroughly blended. Let the batter rest for 2 hours or more. Then stir in enough of the remaining milk to make the batter the consistency of heavy cream.

4. Heat 1 tablespoon oil in a 6-inch crêpe pan or skillet. Pour off any excess oil and add 2 tablespoons of the batter to the center of the hot pan. Tilt the pan so that the batter covers its surface. Cook until the batter forms tiny bubbles and begins to pull away from the outer edge of the pan. Tap the crêpe pan on the outer edge so that the crêpe slides half over the rim away from you. Flip the pan to turn the crêpe. Remove the crêpe to an upturned saucer. Brush the crêpe pan with just enough oil to coat it lightly and continue making crêpes until all the batter is used.

5. Chop the reserved chicken (from step 2 above) very fine.

6. To assemble the crêpes, combine the nutmeg to taste with 1 cup of the Mornay Sauce and stir in the chicken. Add the grated cheese to the remaining sauce and set aside in a covered bowl in the refrigerator.

7. Put 2 tablespoons of the chicken mixture in the middle of each crêpe and roll up the crêpes. Put the filled crêpes, seam side down, in a row in a buttered ovenproof baking dish.

8. Preheat the oven to 450°F.

9. Spoon the reserved Mornay Sauce over the crêpes and bake for 10 minutes, or until the crêpes are slightly browned on top and the sauce is bubbling. Watch them carefully to prevent burning.

ANANAS GLACÉS ORANGE

1 pineapple
1 cup granulated sugar
1 cup water
Grated peel of 1 lemon
4 thin-skinned oranges, peeled and
    sliced

¼ cup brandy
¼ cup orange-flavored liqueur
¼ cup slivered almonds

1. Remove the core and eyes from the pineapple and set them aside.

2. Slice the pineapple into ½-inch-thick slices. Peel and cut into ¼-inch slices.

3. Dissolve the sugar in the water. Add the grated lemon peel and the reserved pineapple core and eyes. Simmer for 10 minutes and strain, discarding the solids.

4. Poach the orange slices in the syrup for 10 minutes. Remove the orange slices with a slotted spoon and set them aside. Let the poaching syrup cool.

5. Layer 3 orange slices overlapping on each pineapple slice.

6. Add the brandy to the poaching syrup and cook until the syrup is light amber colored.

7. Sprinkle the layered fruit with the liqueur, spoon the syrup over, and sprinkle with the almonds. Chill until serving time.

⇓ ⇓ ⇓

THE MENU

Deviled Crab
Chicken Marengo
Simple Green Salad (see page 33)
Apricot Mousse

Deviled Crab, Chicken Marengo, and Apricot Mousse are not for a birdlike appetite or a waist watcher. They appeal to the hearty eater. To lighten this repast I serve a splendid tossed green salad with the entrée and make the servings small. This menu will satisfy the most discerning taste with its varied flavor, color, and texture. Deviled Crab might be served as a luncheon entrée with a simple salad, followed by fresh fruit.

Chicken Marengo is named for the Battle of Marengo in 1800. It is said that Napoleon, in command of the French Army at that time, did not eat until the battle was over. Therefore, we are most grateful for his victory there, which enabled his chef to forage for food from the local farms. If by chance Napoleon had met with defeat, his cook would have been engaged in a hasty retreat, foregoing any culinary experimentation, and thus preventing us from enjoying this dish today.

THE INGREDIENTS

What You Will Need:

1 medium onion
12 small white onions
¼ pound mushrooms
3 tomatoes
2 lemons
1 head Boston lettuce
1 head romaine lettuce
1 bunch parsley sprigs
3½-pound chicken
1 pound lump crabmeat
1 quart milk

¼ pound unsalted butter
½ dozen large eggs
½ pint heavy cream
¼ pound Parmesan cheese
Potato flour
Bread crumbs
½ cup tomato purée
Pitted black olives
6 ounces dried apricots
1 envelope unflavored gelatin
2 tablespoons sunflower seeds

Staples to Have on Hand:

salt, white and black pepper, paprika, dry mustard, Dijon mustard, ground nutmeg, bay leaves, dried thyme, garlic clove, red wine vinegar, olive oil, vegetable oil, Worcestershire sauce, Tabasco, chicken stock (see page 276), flour, granulated sugar, dry white wine

THE WORK SCHEDULE

2 Days Before Serving
1. Check the staples on hand and make your shopping list.
2. Buy everything you will need.
3. Prepare the Chicken Marengo (through step 6 of the recipe), cool, cover, and refrigerate.
4. Soak the apricots overnight (step 1 of the recipe).

1 Day Before Serving
1. Prepare the Apricot Mousse (steps 2 through 4 of the recipe), cover, and refrigerate.
2. Prepare the Deviled Crab (through step 1 of the recipe), cover, and refrigerate.
3. Make the Vinaigrette Dressing (page 282), pour it into a screw-top jar, and refrigerate.
4. Set the table and select the wine.

Serving Day
1. *One half-hour before serving,* preheat the oven to 350°F., top the Deviled Crab with buttered bread crumbs (step 2 of the recipe), and bake for 25 minutes.
2. Reheat the Chicken Marengo in the same oven at the same time. Garnish just before serving (step 8 of the recipe).
3. Prepare the salad greens ready for tossing and refrigerate.
4. Prepare the coffee maker and uncork the wine.

⇟ ⇟ ⇟

DEVILED CRAB

2 teaspoons Worcestershire sauce
2 teaspoons lemon juice
Dash of Tabasco
1 teaspoon salt
½ teaspoon dry mustard
¼ teaspoon white pepper
Ground nutmeg to taste
1½ cups Béchamel Sauce
  (see page 278)

1 pound fresh lump crabmeat
3 tablespoons unsalted butter
½ cup bread crumbs
2 tablespoons grated Parmesan
  cheese
Paprika
2 tablespoons finely chopped parsley

1. Mix the Worcestershire sauce, lemon juice, Tabasco, salt, mustard, pepper, and nutmeg into the Béchamel Sauce. Mix in the crabmeat and pile into ramekins or scallop shells.

2. Melt the butter in a small skillet and stir in the bread crumbs. Stir to coat the bread crumbs with the butter.

3. Preheat the oven to 350°F.

4. Sprinkle the bread crumbs and Parmesan cheese over the crab mixture and bake for 25 minutes. Sprinkle lightly with paprika and chopped parsley before serving.

CHICKEN MARENGO

3 tablespoons vegetable oil
1 3½-pound chicken, cut into 8 serving pieces
1 medium onion, chopped
½ cup tomato purée
2 tablespoons potato flour
2 cups chicken or veal stock (see page 276)
1 cup dry white wine
2 bay leaves
1 clove garlic, crushed with 1 teaspoon salt
1 teaspoon dried thyme
Salt and pepper
12 small white onions
¼ pound mushrooms
3 tomatoes
Pitted black olives, approximately 1 dozen
Finely chopped parsley

1. Preheat the oven to 350°F.

2. Heat the oil in a heavy casserole with a cover. Add the chicken and brown evenly all over.

3. Peel and chop the medium onion; add to the chicken and cook for 3 minutes.

4. Stir in the tomato purée and potato flour and mix thoroughly. Gradually pour in the white wine and part of the stock, reserving enough for step 5. Add the bay leaves, garlic, thyme, and salt and pepper to taste. Cover the casserole and bake in the oven for 15 minutes.

5. Peel the small onions. To do this easily, put them in boiling water for 2 minutes first. Cook the onions until tender in enough reserved stock to cover, then add the onions and stock to the casserole.

6. Wipe the mushrooms clean with a damp cloth and slice them. Peel the tomatoes and cut them into quarters. Add the mushrooms and tomatoes to the casserole and cook, covered, for another 30 minutes, or until the chicken is tender. The length of time will depend on the quality and the age of the chicken. Cool, cover, and refrigerate.

7. One half-hour before serving, return the casserole to a 325°F. oven to reheat.

8. Just before serving, add the olives, and sprinkle with chopped parsley.

APRICOT MOUSSE

6 ounces dried apricots	¼ cup water
2 cups boiling water	2 tablespoons lemon juice
Granulated sugar	1 cup heavy cream
1 envelope unflavored gelatin	5 egg whites

1. Put the apricots in a pan with a tight-fitting lid. Pour the boiling water over them, cover, and let stand—overnight if possible.

2. Simmer the apricots gently until tender. Press through a sieve or purée in a blender until smooth. Add sugar to taste while still hot.

3. Soften the gelatin by sprinkling it over ¼ cup of water. Dissolve over low heat and mix thoroughly with the apricot purée. Stir in the lemon juice. Taste for sweetness and add more sugar if necessary. Chill.

4. Whip the cream until soft peaks form. (If the cream is overbeaten, the mousse will be heavy.) Stir the cream into the chilled purée. Chill again; and when it is setting, beat the egg whites until they hold stiff peaks. Fold the beaten egg whites into the apricot mixture and spoon into ramekins or a soufflé dish. Cover and refrigerate for at least 3 hours.

⇟ ⇟ ⇟

THE MENU

Low-Calorie Vegetable Soup
Chicken Breasts with Green Olives
Rice
Apple Crunch

This chilled vegetable soup is similar to the Spanish gazpacho. I don't believe there is any hard and fast method for preparing gazpacho. Each locality and each family will have its own version and will more than likely use whatever vegetables are available. This particular recipe for cold vegetable soup is not quite so simple as gazpacho, since good chicken stock is used instead of water, making it that much more nourishing. A chicken dish with a Mediterranean flavor and plain boiled or steamed rice follow.

Apple Brown Betty is a simple dessert known to most cooks. The version I use has a different topping which I've named Crunch. It should be served at room temperature with fresh whipped cream, crème fraîche, or sour cream for the more adventurous.

THE INGREDIENTS

What You Will Need:

3 medium carrots
2 celery stalks
2 small onions
1 medium onion
1 pound fine white mushrooms
4 medium tomatoes
1 bunch parsley sprigs

3 pounds cooking apples
3 whole chicken breasts
½ pound unsalted butter
Cooked rice
1 4-ounce bottle pimiento-stuffed
  olives
Dry white wine

Staples to Have on Hand:

salt, pepper, celery salt, paprika, whole cloves, cinnamon sticks, ground ginger, garlic clove, olive oil, vegetable oil, chicken stock (see page 276), baking soda, flour, granulated sugar, light brown sugar, dry vermouth

THE WORK SCHEDULE

3 Days Before Serving
1. Check the staples on hand and make your shopping list.
2. Buy everything you will need.

2 Days Before Serving
1. Prepare the soup (through step 3 of the recipe), cool, cover, and refrigerate.
2. Cook the apples for the dessert (through step 1 of the recipe), cool, cover, and refrigerate.
3. Make the topping for the Apple Crunch (step 2 of the recipe). Put in a screw-top jar and refrigerate.

1 Day Before Serving
1. Prepare the chicken dish, cool, cover, and refrigerate.
2. Set the table and select the wine.

Serving Day
1. *Early in the day*, bake the dessert. It is to be served at room temperature.
2. Chill the bowls or cups for the soup.
3. *Forty minutes before serving*, preheat the oven to 350°F. and reheat the chicken dish for 30 minutes.
4. Cook the rice.
5. Prepare the coffee maker and uncork the wine.

LOW-CALORIE VEGETABLE SOUP

1 tablespoon unsalted butter
3 medium carrots, washed and diced
2 celery stalks, washed and diced
1 small onion, peeled and diced
4 cups chicken stock (see page 276)

¼ teaspoon celery salt
2 or 3 twists of the pepper mill
¼ cup dry vermouth
Finely chopped parsley

1. Melt the butter in a heavy saucepan. Add three-quarters of the diced vegetables, cover the pan, and cook over low heat for 8 minutes, or until the vegetables are soft.

2. Put the vegetables in the blender, add a little of the stock, and purée until smooth. Add the celery salt and pepper to taste and blend to mix.

3. Return the purée to the saucepan. Add the remaining chicken stock, vegetables, and the vermouth, and correct the seasonings. Cool, cover, and refrigerate.

4. Serve with a sprinkling of chopped parsley.

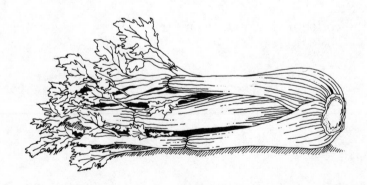

CHICKEN BREASTS WITH GREEN OLIVES

3 whole chicken breasts, halved
1 cup flour
2 teaspoons salt
¼ teaspoon freshly ground pepper
½ teaspoon paprika
½ cup olive oil
1 medium onion, finely chopped
1 clove garlic, finely chopped

1½ cups dry white wine
1 pound white mushrooms
4 medium tomatoes, peeled and quartered
1 4-ounce bottle small pimiento-stuffed olives
Finely chopped parsley

1. Preheat the oven to 350°F.

2. Put the chicken breasts in a paper bag with a mixture of flour, salt, pepper, and paprika. Shake until they are well coated.

3. Heat the oil in a heavy skillet and sauté the onion and garlic until transparent and lightly colored. Remove the onion and garlic and discard. Add the chicken breasts and cook until brown on all sides. Dust with half the remaining seasoned flour in the bag and cook 2 minutes longer.

4. Pour in the white wine and scrape the pan to loosen any bits. Transfer the contents to an ovenproof casserole with a cover.

5. Wipe the mushrooms with a clean damp cloth and slice them very thin.

6. Dip the tomatoes into boiling water for 1 minute, remove the skins, and cut into quarters. Add the mushrooms, tomatoes, and olives to the casserole and bake for 20 minutes, or until the chicken is tender. Cool, cover, and refrigerate.

7. Reheat the chicken in 350°F. oven for 30 minutes.

8. Sprinkle with chopped parsley just before serving. Serve with cooked rice.

⇓ ⇓ ⇓

APPLE CRUNCH

3 pounds cooking apples
⅔ cup plus ¼ cup granulated sugar
½ cup water
6 whole cloves
2 cinnamon sticks
1 stick (4 ounces) unsalted butter, softened

1½ cups flour sifted with a pinch of baking soda and 2 tablespoons ground ginger
¼ cup light brown sugar

1. Peel, core, and slice the apples. Combine with ⅔ cup sugar, water, cloves, and cinnamon and cook until soft. Cool, cover, and refrigerate.

2. Chip the butter into the flour mixture. Crumble with the tips of the fingers until the mixture resembles cornmeal. Add the light brown sugar and the remaining granulated sugar and continue to crumble.

3. Preheat the oven to 350°F.

4. Remove the cloves and cinnamon sticks from the apples and spread the apples over the bottom of a 1½-quart ovenproof dish. Smooth gently but do not pack tight. Spread the topping evenly over the apples, but do not press down. Bake for 30 minutes. Serve at room temperature.

↡ ↡ ↡

THE MENU

Antipasto with Italian Bread
Chicken Breasts en Papillote
Haricots Verts
Lime Sorbet

Antipasto is one of the many splendid creations from Italy. Young vegetables, good wine vinegar, and a tomato sauce worthy of its name contribute to this dish's freshness. Ripe olives, green olives, and strips of red pimiento provide the color. It keeps well when refrigerated. Served with crusty fresh Italian bread, Antipasto makes a good luncheon dish on a hot summer day, followed by fresh fruit and cheese.

Papillote or envelope-cooking is an old method. Banana leaves were among the earliest envelopes that spring to mind. They have the unique advantage of leaving the oven as clean at the end of baking time as it was at the start.

The balance of color, texture, and flavor of this menu is achieved by the selection of lime sorbet for dessert.

THE INGREDIENTS

What You Will Need:

1 celery stalk
¼ pound small mushrooms
12 small white onions
2 pounds young green beans
2 carrots
1 small head cauliflower
2 small green peppers
1 small eggplant
1 large bunch mint leaves
2 lemons

5 to 6 limes
6 chicken breast halves
⅓ pound boiled ham
3 large eggs
½ pound unsalted butter
Italian bread
Green olives
Ripe olives
Pimientos
6 sheets (16 by 15 inches) parchment
    paper

Staples to Have on Hand:

salt, pepper, bay leaf, dry mustard, garlic clove, olive oil, red wine vinegar,
ketchup, granulated sugar, green food coloring

THE WORK SCHEDULE

3 Days Before Serving
1. Check the staples on hand and make your shopping list.
2. Buy everything you will need with the exception of the chicken breasts.

2 Days Before Serving
1. Buy the chicken breasts and refrigerate.
2. Prepare the Antipasto. Cool, cover, and refrigerate.
3. Prepare the Mint Butter (see page 283) for the Chicken Breasts en Papillote.

1 Day Before Serving
1. Prepare the Chicken Breasts en Papillote (through step 2 of the recipe) and refrigerate.
2. Prepare the syrup and lime juice for the sorbet (through step 2 of the recipe). Cover and refrigerate.
3. Wash and prepare the Haricots Verts (through step 3 of the recipe). Dry, cover, and refrigerate.
4. Set the table and select the wine.

Serving Day
1. *In the late afternoon,* freeze the sorbet (steps 3 and 4 of the recipe). When finished, remove the dasher, tamp down the mixture, wrap the freezing can in newspaper to prevent it from becoming too hard, and place it in the freezing compartment of the refrigerator.
2. Chill the glasses or plates for the sorbet.
3. *One hour before serving,* arrange the Antipasto on a suitable serving dish. Let it come to room temperature.
4. *Forty minutes before serving,* preheat the oven to 350°F. in readiness for cooking the papillotes. Brush them with the beaten egg and bake for 30 minutes (steps 3 and 4 of the recipe).
5. *Fifteen minutes before serving,* melt the butter in a skillet in readiness for reheating the green beans.
6. Prepare the coffee maker and uncork the wine.

⇟ ⇟ ⇟

ANTIPASTO

1 cup olive oil
1 clove garlic, coarsely chopped
1 bay leaf
1 celery stalk, cut into 1-inch lengths
¼ pound small mushrooms, trimmed
  and quartered
12 small white onions, peeled and
  quartered
¼ pound green beans, broken into
  pieces
2 carrots, scraped and cut into
  1-inch lengths

1 small head cauliflower, broken
  into bite-sized pieces
2 small green peppers, seeded and
  cut into thin strips
1 small eggplant, unpeeled, cubed
8 large green olives
12 large ripe olives
3 pimientos, cut into broad strips
1 cup ketchup
1 cup red wine vinegar
2 tablespoons granulated sugar
1 tablespoon dry mustard
Salt and pepper

1. In a large saucepan heat the olive oil. Stir in the garlic and cook until the garlic is golden. Remove the garlic and discard.

2. Add the bay leaf, celery, mushrooms, onions, green beans, carrots, cauliflower, green peppers, and eggplant to the hot oil. Cook, uncovered, until the vegetables are tender but still crisp.

3. Stir in the olives, pimientos, ketchup, vinegar, sugar, mustard, and salt and pepper to taste. Cook for 15 minutes, stirring frequently. Cool. Cover and refrigerate before serving with crusty bread.

CHICKEN BREASTS EN PAPILLOTE

Melted unsalted butter
6 chicken breast halves, boned and
  sliced in half horizontally
⅓ pound boiled ham, finely chopped

Mint Butter (see page 283)
Salt and pepper
2 eggs, lightly beaten

1. Fold each sheet of parchment in half and open it up again. Brush the paper with melted butter. Lay a chicken breast on one half of each piece of paper. Smooth equal portions of the chopped ham on one half of each breast. Dot with Mint Butter and fold the other half of the breast over. Season the chicken breasts with salt and pepper.

2. Fold the parchment paper over the breast and brush the edges of the paper with beaten egg. Start rolling the paper tightly from one corner to make a well-sealed package. Brush the whole package with melted butter. Refrigerate.

3. Preheat the oven to 350°F. Brush the papillotes with the beaten egg.

4. Bake for 30 minutes. Slide the breast out of the package onto a plate and serve with Haricots Verts.

⇓ ⇓ ⇓

HARICOTS VERTS

1½ pounds very fresh young green
  beans
Boiling salted water

1 to 2 tablespoons unsalted butter (as
  little as possible)

1. Cover the beans with cold water for 1 hour. Drain.

2. Trim the beans by cutting off both ends. If the beans are extra long, cut them in half on the bias with scissors.

(Continued)

3. Bring the water to a rolling boil and drop the beans in by the handful. When the water comes to a boil again, drop in a second handful, and so on. Cook for 3 to 4 minutes and test for doneness by biting into a bean. When cooked just *al dente*, drain the beans and run them under cold water to stop the cooking process and bring back the color. Dry thoroughly, cover, and refrigerate.

4. Just before serving, melt the butter in a skillet and toss the beans in the hot butter until heated.

LIME SORBET

1 cup granulated sugar
2 cups hot water
1 cup lime juice

1 egg white
2 drops green food coloring

1. Dissolve the sugar in the hot water over low heat. Bring to a boil. Lower the heat, and simmer for approximately 5 minutes, or until the temperature on a candy thermometer reads 216°F.

2. Cool, stir in the lime juice, and chill thoroughly.

3. Freeze in a mechanical freezer (I use the Waring's Ice Cream Parlor) for 20 minutes, or until the mixture resembles melted snow—slushlike.

4. Beat the egg white and fold it and the food coloring into the lime slush. Continue freezing for 20 minutes, or longer, if needed.

↯↯↯

THE MENU

Pannequet de Saumon Fumé
Virginia Baked Chicken
Simple Green Salad (see page 33)
Meringues

The Pannequet de Saumon Fumé is rich and unusual and well worth trying. Virginia Baked Chicken is a dish I have served at luncheons and taken on picnics with equal success. If small drumsticks are available, I cook them following this recipe and serve them at cocktail parties when substantial food is required.

Meringue has a host of uses, but the version I prefer above all others has a filling of unsweetened whipped cream—a schoolday favorite of mine.

THE INGREDIENTS

What You Will Need:

1 head Boston lettuce
1 head romaine lettuce
1 bunch parsley
1 lemon
¼ pound thinly sliced smoked salmon
1 large broiling chicken
½ dozen large eggs

½ pound unsalted butter
½ pint sour cream
1 pint heavy cream or 1 quart ice cream
Milk
Seasoned bread crumbs (see Note page 93)
2 tablespoons sunflower seeds

Staples to Have on Hand:

salt, pepper, cream of tartar, almond extract, olive oil, vegetable oil, red wine vinegar, Dijon mustard, flour, granulated sugar

⇊ ⇊ ⇊

THE WORK SCHEDULE

3 Days Before Serving

1. Check the staples on hand and make your shopping list.
2. Buy everything you will need with the exception of the salmon, chicken, salad greens, and heavy cream or ice cream.
3. Prepare the Meringues and wrap and freeze them.

2 Days Before Serving

1. Buy the salmon, chicken, salad greens, and heavy cream or ice cream.
2. Prepare the crêpes for the Pannequet (through step 2 of the recipe), wrap, and freeze them.

1 Day Before Serving

1. Prepare the chicken completely. Cool, cover, and refrigerate.
2. Make the Vinaigrette Dressing (see page 282) and store in a screw-top jar in the refrigerator.
3. Set the table and select the wine.

Serving Day

1. *Two hours before serving,* take the chicken out of the refrigerator and the Meringues out of the freezer.
2. *One hour before serving,* make the Hollandaise Sauce for the Pannequet (see page 279) and stand it in tepid water until needed.
3. *Forty-five minutes before serving,* preheat the oven to 350°F. Assemble the salmon-stuffed crêpes (through step 4 of the recipe) and bake for 20 minutes.
4. Put the chicken in the oven at the same time as the stuffed crêpes and heat for 30 minutes.
5. Whip the cream and fill the Meringues. Refrigerate until serving time.
6. Prepare the salad greens ready for tossing and refrigerate.
7. *Just before serving,* spoon the Hollandaise Sauce over the filled crêpes and glaze under the broiler.
8. Prepare the coffee maker and uncork the wine.

↓↓↓

PANNEQUET DE SAUMON FUMÉ

1½ cups flour
½ teaspoon salt
2½ cups milk
2 tablespoons vegetable oil
2 eggs
2 egg yolks

Oil for cooking
¼ pound thinly sliced smoked salmon, coarsely chopped
Hollandaise Sauce (see page 279)
½ cup parsley sprigs, chopped

1. In a bowl combine the flour, salt, and ½ cup milk. Add the 2 tablespoons oil while beating. Continue to beat while adding the eggs and egg yolks. Beat the batter until it is smooth and thoroughly blended. Let it rest for 2 hours or more. Then stir in enough of the remaining milk to make the batter the consistency of heavy cream.

2. Heat 1 tablespoon oil in a 6-inch crêpe pan or skillet. Pour off any excess oil and add 2 tablespoons of the batter to the center of the hot pan. Tilt the pan so that the batter covers its surface. Cook until the batter forms tiny bubbles and begins to leave the outer edge of the pan. Tap the crêpe pan on the outer edge so that the crêpe slides half over the rim away from you. Flip the pan to turn the crêpe. Remove the crêpe to an upturned saucer. Brush the crêpe pan with just enough oil to coat it lightly, and continue making crêpes until all the batter is used.

3. Combine the chopped salmon with ½ cup Hollandaise Sauce. Use approximately 1 tablespoon of the mixture to fill each of 12 crêpes, turning in the sides and rolling them neatly.

4. Butter a shallow ovenproof dish and arrange the filled crêpes seam side down in the dish.

5. Preheat the oven to 350°F.

6. Heat in the oven for 20 minutes. Spread generously with the remaining Hollandaise Sauce and glaze under the broiler until the sauce bubbles. Sprinkle with chopped parsley before serving.

VIRGINIA BAKED CHICKEN

1 broiling chicken, cut into 8 pieces ½ cup seasoned bread crumbs (see
1 cup sour cream   Note)
    Melted butter

1. Preheat the oven to 375°F.

2. Skin the chicken pieces and put them in a shallow dish. Cover each piece completely with sour cream.

3. Lift the chicken pieces from the sour cream one by one and roll in the bread crumbs. As each piece is crumbed, place it on an oiled baking sheet.

4. Dribble the melted butter over each piece of chicken and bake for 45 minutes.

Note: If you prefer to make your own seasoned bread crumbs, you can add 1 teaspoon salt, ¼ teaspoon pepper, and 1 teaspoon dried thyme to 2 cups of bread crumbs.

⇊ ⇊ ⇊

MERINGUES

½ cup (3 to 3½) egg whites 1 cup granulated sugar
Pinch of salt 1 tablespoon almond extract
Pinch of cream of tartar 1 pint heavy cream, or 1 quart ice
    cream

1. Preheat the oven to 225°F.

2. Beat the egg whites with an electric mixer until they foam. Add the salt and the cream of tartar. Beat a little faster until the whites hold shape. Continue to beat and add the sugar 1 tablespoon at a time, beating after each addition.

(Continued)

Add the almond extract when half the sugar has been used. Continue beating and adding sugar until all the sugar is used. Increase the speed again and beat for about 8 minutes, or until very stiff and the sugar is dissolved.

3. Spoon the meringue (or use a pastry bag fitted with a plain or fluted nozzle) onto a cookie sheet lined with parchment paper or aluminum foil. Bake for 1 hour.

4. Turn off the oven and open the oven door. Allow the meringues to dry out in the oven for 1 hour.

5. To serve, fill with flavored whipped cream or ice cream. Makes about 20 large meringues.

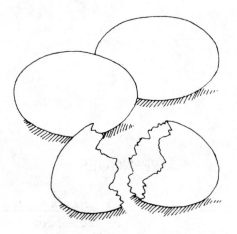

⇟⇟⇟

THE MENU

Mousse of Ham
Chicken Florentine
Your Favorite Green Salad with Vinaigrette Dressing
Madeleines

To make a menu such as this even more memorable, all that is needed is something delicious like Madeleines to nibble on with coffee. I would recommend making the Mousse of Ham in small ramekins rather than in a 6-cup mold. There will be little risk, then, that guests will overindulge because they like the mousse and consequently have little appetite for the splendid chicken dish. A tossed green salad with the entrée would not be out of place.

THE INGREDIENTS

What You Will Need:

3 shallots
2 carrots
2 celery stalks
1 onion
Salad greens
2 pounds spinach
1 bunch parsley sprigs
3 large lemons
1¼ pounds boiled ham, ground

4 whole chicken breasts
½ dozen large eggs
½ pound unsalted butter
½ pint heavy cream
2 ounces Gruyère cheese
1 ounce Parmesan cheese
2 envelopes unflavored gelatin
1 madeleine pan

Staples to Have on Hand:

  salt, pepper, cayenne, ground nutmeg, dried thyme, bay leaf, Dijon mustard, olive oil, red wine vinegar, chicken stock (see page 276), tomato paste, dry bread crumbs, flour, granulated sugar, vanilla extract, dry vermouth, dry Madeira

THE WORK SCHEDULE

3 Days Before Serving
1. Check the staples on hand and make your shopping list.
2. Buy everything you will need.

2 Days Before Serving
1. Decide how you will serve the Mousse of Ham, making sure you have sufficient ramekins of the right size. I would suggest ½-cup ramekins.
2. Prepare the mousse, cover, and refrigerate.
3. Bake the Madeleines and store them in an airtight container.

1 Day Before Serving
1. Prepare the Chicken Florentine (through step 6 of the recipe), cool, wrap in plastic, and refrigerate.
2. Set the table and select the wine.
3. Make the Vinaigrette Dressing (page 282), pour it in a screw-top jar, and refrigerate.

Serving Day
1. *Four or five hours before serving,* take the Chicken Florentine out of the refrigerator to give it time to reach room temperature.
2. *Three hours before serving,* unmold the mousse onto a suitable platter and refrigerate until serving time.
3. Arrange the Madeleines on a serving plate.
4. Arrange the salad ready for tossing at the last minute.
5. *One half-hour before serving,* preheat the oven to 350°F. and warm the Chicken Florentine for 20 minutes. Then brown under broiler.
6. Prepare the coffee maker and uncork the wine.

↯ ↯ ↯

MOUSSE OF HAM

3 tablespoons finely chopped shallots
1 tablespoon unsalted butter
2 cups chicken stock (see page 276)
2 envelopes unflavored gelatin softened in ¼ cup dry vermouth
1 tablespoon tomato paste

2⅓ cups ground boiled ham
Salt, pepper, and ground nutmeg to taste
3 tablespoons dry Madeira
2 tablespoons lemon juice
Grated peel of 1 lemon
¾ cup heavy cream

1. Cook shallots slowly in butter until soft, taking care they do not brown; otherwise the flavor will change. Add chicken stock, gelatin mixture, and tomato paste. Blend until smooth. Add ground ham half at a time. (I find the blender produces a very fine purée.)

2. Empty into a clean bowl to cool. Season with salt, pepper, and nutmeg. Season more than you would think necessary; the cream will tone it down. Add the Madeira, lemon juice, and lemon peel.

3. When almost set, whip the cream until soft peaks form and fold into the setting ham mixture. Correct the seasonings and spoon into the prepared mold or ramekins.

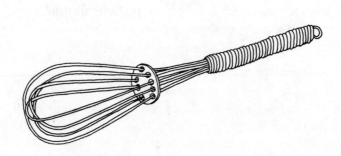

CHICKEN FLORENTINE

2 carrots, coarsely chopped
2 celery stalks, coarsely chopped
½ onion, coarsely chopped
½ bay leaf
¼ teaspoon dried thyme
Salt and pepper
1¾ cups chicken stock (see page 276)
4 whole chicken breasts
3 tablespoons butter
3 tablespoons flour

2 pounds spinach
Ground nutmeg to taste
2 egg yolks, beaten
¼ cup heavy cream
2 tablespoons lemon juice
Pinch of cayenne
½ cup grated Gruyère cheese
2 tablespoons grated Parmesan cheese
Chopped parsley

1. Preheat the oven to 400°F.

2. Butter an ovenproof dish thoroughly. Make a bed of the chopped vegetables; add the bay leaf and thyme and season with salt and pepper. Pour the chicken stock over the vegetables. Lay the chicken breasts on top and sprinkle with salt and pepper. Cover with well-buttered wax paper and bake for 40 minutes.

3. Lift out the chicken breasts. Drain the juices; there should be 2 cups. Remove the bones from the chicken breasts. Slice in scallops.

4. Melt 3 tablespoons butter in a saucepan. Add 3 tablespoons flour and blend. Add the vegetable stock and simmer gently for 30 minutes, stirring from time to time.

5. Blanch the spinach and drain thoroughly. Season with salt, pepper, nutmeg and butter.

6. Butter an ovenproof dish. Make a bed of the spinach. Lay the sliced chicken on top. Mix the egg yolks and cream and stir into the sauce to thicken. Add the lemon juice and cayenne. Pour over chicken. Scatter the cheese on top. Cool, wrap in plastic, and refrigerate.

7. Reheat in 350°F. oven for 20 minutes until hot, and then brown under broiler. Sprinkle with chopped parsley.

MADELEINES

¼ cup plus 1½ tablespoons unsalted butter, softened
Dry bread crumbs
1 egg plus 2 egg yolks, at room temperature
¼ cup granulated sugar
½ teaspoon vanilla extract
½ cup sifted flour
Finely grated peel of 1 large lemon

1. Adjust rack to one-third from bottom of oven. Preheat the oven to 375°F. To prepare the pan, brush 1½ tablespoons butter on the forms, brushing from the top to the bottom the long way and then reversing and brushing from the bottom to the top. Examine the forms carefully to make sure that you haven't missed any spots and also that the butter is not too thick anywhere. Now, over paper, sprinkle the forms with fine dry bread crumbs. Tilt and shake the pan to coat the forms thoroughly. Invert the pan and tap it firmly, leaving a very light coating of crumbs.

2. Cut up the ¼ cup of butter and, in a small pan over low heat, melt it, stirring occasionally. Set aside to cool but do not let it harden.

3. In a small bowl of an electric mixer beat the egg, egg yolks, sugar, and vanilla at high speed for about 15 minutes, or until the mixture barely flows when beaters are lifted. On lowest speed gradually add the flour, scraping the bowl with a rubber spatula as necessary and beating only until the flour is incorporated—do not overbeat. Remove from mixer. (Use your fingertips to remove the batter from the beaters.)

4. Fold in the lemon peel and then, in four or five additions, the cooled butter, folding only until no butter shows. Bake immediately—do not let the batter stand.

5. Spoon the batter into the prepared forms. The batter will be mounded slightly above the tops of the forms. Do not smooth; the batter will level itself.

6. Bake for 18 minutes, or until the tops are golden brown and spring back firmly when lightly touched. If necessary, reverse the position of the pan for the last few minutes of baking to ensure even browning. The Madeleines must be removed from the pan immediately. Quickly cover the pan with a rack or a cookie sheet and invert. Remove the pan. Cool the Madeleines on a rack.

⇟ ⇟ ⇟

THE MENU

Eggplant Caviar with French Bread
Chicken Cacciatore
Blueberry Grunt

I'm not quite sure where Eggplant Caviar originated, but it is so good and, for this day and age, inexpensive that its origin does not matter. Served as a first course or with cocktails, it is a winner. Not too rich, it is a stimulator of gastric juices, and a perfect introduction to Chicken Cacciatore.

Blueberry Grunt made the blueberry a friend to my palate. Until I found this all-American dish soon after my arrival in this country, I thought that blueberries were rather insipid and flavorless. But I was quickly converted by this humble-sounding dessert.

THE INGREDIENTS

What You Will Need:

2 1-pound eggplants	6 chicken breasts
1 small onion	6 chicken legs
2 medium onions	½ pound unsalted butter
1 green pepper	2 1-pound, 3-ounce cans Italian
1 bunch parsley sprigs	plum tomatoes
5 lemons	1 8-ounce can tomato sauce
3 pints blueberries	1 loaf of French bread

Staples to Have on Hand:

   salt, celery salt, pepper, bay leaf, dried oregano, garlic cloves, olive oil, vegetable oil, flour, dark brown sugar

THE WORK SCHEDULE

3 Days Before Serving
1. Check the staples on hand and make your shopping list.
2. Buy everything you will need with the exception of the chicken, blueberries, and French bread.

2 Days Before Serving
1. Buy the chicken and the blueberries.
2. Prepare the Eggplant Caviar, cover, and refrigerate.

1 Day Before Serving
1. Prepare the Chicken Cacciatore (through step 4 of the recipe). Cool, cover, and refrigerate.
2. Make the topping for the Blueberry Grunt (step 1 of the recipe), cover, and refrigerate.
3. Wash and clean the blueberries. Drain well and refrigerate until Serving Day.
4. Set the table and select the wine.

Serving Day
1. Buy the French bread.
2. *Five hours before serving,* take the chicken out of the refrigerator.
3. *Four hours before serving,* arrange the blueberries in an au gratin dish and cover with the topping.
4. *Three hours before serving,* bake the Blueberry Grunt for 20 minutes, but do not refrigerate it again. Serve it at room temperature.
5. *One hour before serving,* arrange the Eggplant Caviar on a serving dish. A dish of unsalted butter should accompany the French bread.
6. *Forty minutes before serving,* preheat the oven to 350°F. Warm the chicken for 30 minutes. Sauté the green pepper and add to the chicken dish for the last 10 minutes of cooking (steps 5 and 6 of the recipe).
7. Prepare the coffee maker and uncork the wine.

☟ ☟ ☟

EGGPLANT CAVIAR

2 1-pound eggplants
Salt
1 small onion, finely chopped
2 cloves garlic, finely chopped
½ cup parsley sprigs, finely chopped

¼ cup lemon juice
¼ cup olive oil
Pepper
1 loaf of French bread

1. Cut the eggplants in half and make cuts on the cut side. Sprinkle with salt and let stand for 1 hour, then rinse and pat dry with paper towels.

2. Preheat the oven to 375°F.

3. Put the eggplants cut-side down on an oiled baking sheet and bake for 40 minutes.

4. When the eggplants are cool enough to handle, scoop out the pulp and chop it. Add the onion, garlic, and parsley. Beat in the lemon juice and olive oil. Season with salt and pepper to taste. Cover and refrigerate. Serve at room temperature with French bread.

⇊ ⇊ ⇊

CHICKEN CACCIATORE

2 medium onions, chopped
Oil for sautéing
2 medium cloves garlic, peeled and
   crushed
6 whole chicken breasts, cut in half
6 chicken legs, cut in half
2 1-pound, 3-ounce cans imported
   Italian plum tomatoes

1 8-ounce can tomato sauce
1 bay leaf
½ teaspoon celery salt
½ teaspoon dried oregano
Salt and pepper
1 green pepper, seeded and diced

1. Sauté the onions in the olive oil until they are transparent. Add the garlic for the last few minutes. Remove the onions from the pan and set aside.

2. Add the chicken to the oil in the pan and sauté the chicken on all sides until golden brown. Remove the chicken and set aside.

3. Preheat the oven to 400°F.

4. Combine the tomatoes, tomato sauce, onions, bay leaf, celery salt, oregano, and salt and pepper to taste in an ovenproof pot. Heat for approximately 10 minutes, or until the tomatoes start to break up. Add the chicken to the sauce and bake for 1½ to 1¾ hours. Cool, cover, and refrigerate.

5. When ready to serve, warm the chicken in a 350°F. oven for about 30 minutes.

6. Sauté the green pepper in a little oil and add to the chicken for the last 10 minutes of cooking.

⚡⚡⚡

BLUEBERRY GRUNT

1½ cups flour
¾ cup unsalted butter
2½ cups dark brown sugar

3 pints blueberries, picked over, washed, and drained

1. Blend the flour and butter until the mixture resembles coarse cornmeal. Mix with the sugar, cover, and refrigerate until needed.

2. Preheat the oven to 375°F.

3. Put the blueberries in a well-buttered au gratin dish. Crumble the topping over the blueberries and bake for 20 minutes. Serve at room temperature.

⚡⚡⚡

⚛ ⚛ ⚛

THE MENU

Tapenade
French Bread and Unsalted Butter
Salad Argentine
Chocolate Mousse

Tapenade, Salad Argentine—a roast beef and vegetable salad—followed by a small portion of rich Chocolate Mousse never fails to please guests on a hot summer's night. It is a simple menu to put together and easy to serve. When the meal is accompanied by vin rosé from the South of France, an atmosphere as rosy as the wine is created.

If the Tapenade is too garlicky, cut down on the number of cloves. This is a powerful spread, but serving it with unsalted butter and crusty French bread tempers it.

The Chocolate Mousse is an old favorite. I like to call it my one-one-one recipe: one of each—egg, chocolate, and so on. It can be increased in quantity successfully and has the additional advantage of improving in flavor when it is made a day ahead of time.

THE INGREDIENTS

What You Will Need:

1½ pounds green beans
1 bunch parsley sprigs
2 lemons
Lettuce
2 pounds sirloin of beef
Large eggs

Unsalted butter
Sour cream
Anchovies
2 cups pitted Greek or Italian olives
Semisweet chocolate
1 loaf of French bread

Staples to Have on Hand:

   salt, coarse salt, pepper, garlic cloves, capers, olive oil, red wine vinegar, Dijon mustard, granulated sugar, brandy, dark rum

THE WORK SCHEDULE

2 Days Before Serving

1. Check the staples on hand and make your shopping list.
2. Decide on how many portions of Chocolate Mousse you will make and buy ingredients accordingly. Buy everything you will need with the exception of the green beans and French bread.
3. Roast the beef to the desired doneness (rare, medium, or well done). Cool, cover, and refrigerate.

1 Day Before Serving

1. Buy the green beans and cook them in salted boiling water until *al dente*. Drain, dry well, cover, and refrigerate.
2. Prepare the Tapenade, cover, and refrigerate.
3. Prepare the Chocolate Mousse, cover, and refrigerate.
4. Set the table and select the wine.

Serving Day

1. Buy the French bread.
2. *One hour before serving,* make the dressing for the Salad Argentine (step 1 of the recipe) and refrigerate.
3. *One hour before serving,* arrange the Tapenade for serving. Cut the bread and put out the butter at the last minute.
4. Prepare the coffee maker and uncork the wine.
5. *Fifteen minutes before serving,* slice and julienne the beef and complete the salad.
6. Serve the Chocolate Mousse directly from the refrigerator.

TAPENADE

8 anchovies, drained and rinsed in hot water
1 tablespoon capers
2 small cloves garlic, crushed to a paste with a little coarse salt
2 cups pitted Greek or Italian olives

2 tablespoons lemon juice
¼ cup olive oil, approximately
2 tablespoons brandy
Salt
2 to 3 twists of the pepper mill

Blend the anchovies and capers in a food processor or blender. Add the garlic paste, olives, and lemon juice. Blend for 30 seconds longer. Add enough olive oil to make a paste. Season with the brandy and salt and pepper to taste. Serve at room temperature with unsalted butter and French bread.

⚓ ⚓ ⚓

SALAD ARGENTINE

1½ tablespoons red wine vinegar
6 tablespoons olive oil
2 tablespoons lemon juice
½ teaspoon salt
4 tablespoons sour cream
2 tablespoons Dijon mustard

Pepper
1½ pounds cooked green beans
2 pounds sirloin of beef, roasted, sliced, and cut into julienne
Lettuce leaves
Finely chopped parsley

1. Make the dressing by combining the vinegar, oil, lemon juice, salt, sour cream, mustard, and pepper to taste in a screw-top jar.

2. Mix the beans and beef with enough dressing to coat generously. Serve on lettuce leaves sprinkled with parsley.

⚓ ⚓ ⚓

CHOCOLATE MOUSSE

This recipe makes 1 generous serving. Increase the ingredients for the number of servings needed.

1 ounce semisweet chocolate	1 teaspoon granulated sugar
1 teaspoon unsalted butter	½ teaspoon dark rum
1 egg, separated	

1. Melt the chocolate and butter in the top of a double boiler over simmering water. Cool slightly.

2. Beat the egg yolk and stir it into the chocolate mixture.

3. Beat the egg white until almost stiff. Add the sugar and beat until definite peaks are formed. Fold in the rum.

4. Fold the beaten egg white into the chocolate mixture and spoon the mousse into a ramekin. Cover and refrigerate.

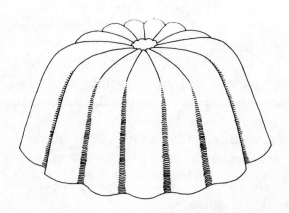

⚡ ⚡ ⚡

THE MENU

Salad Romano
Roulade of Beef
Vegetable Mélange
Oranges and Cracked Caramel

This menu is well worth the time and trouble it takes to prepare; and once the preparation is completed, you can decide whether to serve the roulade hot or cold. If the latter is your choice, substitute a soup for the Salad Romano, and serve a salad of ultra *al dente* green beans tossed in a simple vinaigrette dressing. The orange segments with cracked caramel come as a surprise in both flavor and texture. Don't be put off by the caramel's close resemblance to amber-colored glass—you are among friends.

THE INGREDIENTS

What You Will Need:

2 carrots
3 celery stalks
¾ pound firm white mushrooms
1 small celery root
2 small turnips
½ pound very young green beans
3 small zucchini
1 lemon

1 bunch watercress
1 bunch parsley
3 thin-skinned oranges
2½ pounds flank steak
½ pound unsalted butter
¼ pound Gruyère cheese
½ pint heavy cream
12 slices firm white bread

Staples to Have on Hand:

   salt, pepper, vegetable seasoning salt, dried sage, olive oil, vegetable oil, red wine vinegar, Dijon mustard, beef stock (see page 275), flour, granulated sugar, dry Marsala

THE WORK SCHEDULE

3 Days Before Serving

1. Check the staples on hand and make your shopping list.
2. Buy everything you will need with the exception of the flank steak, parsley, and mushrooms.

2 Days Before Serving

1. Buy the steak, parsley, and mushrooms.
2. If the butcher has not already done so, trim the steak of all membranes and most of the fat. Then split or "butterfly" it lengthwise, following the grain, but leave the steak all in one piece (step 1 of the recipe). Cover and refrigerate.
3. Prepare the Vinaigrette Dressing (see page 282) and store in a screw-top jar in the refrigerator.
4. Peel and slice the oranges (step 1 of the recipe). Cover and refrigerate.

1 Day Before Serving

1. Prepare the roulade and cook through step 6 of the recipe. Cool, cover, and refrigerate.
2. Julienne the vegetables for the mélange. Put in plastic bags and refrigerate.
3. Julienne the cheese and celery for the Salad Romano. Cover and refrigerate.
4. Prepare the cracked caramel (step 2 of the recipe). Store in a jar to maintain the caramel's crispness.
5. Set the table and select the wine.

Serving Day

1. *Two hours before serving*, take the roulade out of the refrigerator.
2. *Forty-five minutes before serving*, preheat the oven to 350°F. and warm the roulade for 30 minutes and complete steps 8 through 10 of the recipe.
3. *One half-hour before serving*, dress the Salad Romano.
4. Assemble the dessert (step 3 of the recipe) and refrigerate until serving time.
5. *Ten minutes before serving*, prepare the green beans for the Mélange and remove the watercress stem. Heat the butter and oil in a wok and cook the vegetables, stirring in the watercress leaves at the last minute.
6. Prepare the coffee maker and uncork the wine.

SALAD ROMANO

¼ pound Gruyère cheese
3 celery stalks
3 or 4 medium mushrooms

Vinaigrette Dressing (see page 282)
1 tablespoon finely chopped parsley

1. Slice the cheese very thin and cut into julienne strips about 1½ inches long.

2. Wash and scrape the celery if necessary. Cut the stalks into 1½-inch-long sections, then julienne.

3. Wipe the mushrooms with a damp cloth and slice very thin.

4. Combine the cheese, celery, and mushrooms in a salad bowl. Add the Vinaigrette Dressing and toss lightly. Allow to stand for 15 to 20 minutes before serving. Garnish with chopped parsley.

⚜ ⚜ ⚜

ROULADE OF BEEF

1 2½-pound flank steak
½ pound firm white mushrooms
1 cup parsley sprigs, packed down
1 teaspoon dried sage
6 cups fresh white bread crumbs,
    made from 12 slices of firm bread

½ cup unsalted butter, melted
Salt and pepper
½ cup dry Marsala
2 tablespoons vegetable oil
1 cup beef stock (see page 275)
Flour

1. Trim the steak of all membranes and most of the fat, then split or "butterfly" lengthwise, following the grain of the meat. Do not cut all the way through, but leave the steak in one piece. (If you are not up to this, ask your butcher to do it.)

2. Wipe the caps of the mushrooms with a clean damp cloth and snip off the tips of the stems. Chop the mushrooms very fine. Mince the parsley.

3. Combine the mushrooms, parsley, sage, bread crumbs, butter, salt and pepper to taste, and ¼ cup Marsala. Mix thoroughly with your hands.

4. Spread the stuffing over the steak, leaving a margin of about ½ inch all around. Roll the steak up with the grain but not too tightly. Tie in several places with fine soft string.

5. Preheat the oven to 350°F.

6. Heat the oil in a large heavy skillet and brown the roulade on all sides. Use tongs or 2 wooden spoons to turn the roulade—a fork will puncture the roll. Put the browned roulade in a roasting pan and add ½ cup beef stock. Dust the roulade with flour. Roast for 25 minutes, turning three or four times. Add the remaining stock and Marsala and roast for 10 minutes longer—a total of 35 minutes. Cool, cover, and refrigerate.

7. Preheat oven to 350°F. and bake the roulade uncovered for 30 minutes, or until warmed through.

8. Remove the roulade to a heated serving platter, cut and discard the strings, and keep the roulade warm.

9. If there isn't sufficient liquid in the pan to sauce the meat, add a little boiling water to the roasting pan and put the pan over medium heat. Scrape the sides and bottom of the pan with a wooden spoon to incorporate all the rich browned-on bits. Strain the sauce over the meat.

10. To serve, cut the roulade as you would a jelly roll.

Note: This roulade is equally delicious served cold, accompanied by green beans dressed with Vinaigrette Dressing.

VEGETABLE MÉLANGE

Unsalted butter and vegetable oil in
   equal quantities
2 carrots, julienned
1 small celery root, or 2 celery stalks,
   julienned
2 small turnips, julienned

½ pound very young green beans,
   topped and tailed
3 small zucchini, julienned
1 teaspoon vegetable seasoning salt
1 handful watercress leaves

1. Heat 1 tablespoon butter and 1 tablespoon oil in a wok. Add the carrots, celery root, turnips, and beans. Cook over high heat, stirring constantly. Test now and again and, as soon as the rawness begins to disappear, add the zucchini and the seasoning salt. Cook and stir for 1 or 2 minutes longer.

2. Just before serving, stir in the watercress. Serve immediately.

⇊ ⇊ ⇊

ORANGES AND CRACKED CARAMEL

3 thin-skinned oranges
1 cup granulated sugar

¾ cup water
1 cup heavy cream

1. Peel the oranges and make neat segments, removing all pith. Be careful not to lose any of the juice. Chill the orange segments.

2. Bring the sugar and water to a boil, reduce the heat, and simmer until the syrup turns a dark amber color. Pour the syrup in a thin stream onto a lightly oiled baking sheet. When cool, chip the caramel off the sheet and set aside.

3. Just before serving, whip the heavy cream and use it to coat the orange segments. Scatter caramel chips on top of each serving.

⇊ ⇊ ⇊

⇟⇟⇟

THE MENU

Cream of Celery Soup
Pâté de Viande (Meat Loaf de Luxe)
Vegetable Salad
Pecan Meringue Torte

Through the summer months I spend out in the country, I try to do most of my cooking either in the early morning or after the sun goes down. Invariably, the daytime hours are spent out-of-doors.

I like to make use of the cornucopia of vegetables and fruits available during those months. A vegetable soup, vegetable salad, and strawberry filling for the torte are the mainstays of this menu.

The pâté (although this is a meat loaf, my students prefer to call it pâté, finding meat loaf too mundane) is rarely consumed at one sitting. The leftovers come in handy for sandwiches the following day.

Use your imagination when making a salad selection and choose available vegetables when they are at their best. Bon appétit!

THE INGREDIENTS

What You Will Need:

1 head celery
3 celery stalks
1 knob celeriac
3 medium onions
10 ounces green beans
4 carrots
½ small head cauliflower
¼ pound mushrooms
Small green pepper
Lettuce
1 lemon
1 bunch parsley
Fresh strawberries

1 cup raspberries or 6 tablespoons
   apricot purée
2 pounds ground top round or sirloin
1 pound ground veal
1 pound ground pork
8 ounces cottage cheese
½ dozen large eggs
½ pint heavy cream
½ cup bottled chili sauce
8 ounces tomato sauce
1 cup bread crumbs
1 cup chopped pecans
Parchment paper

Staples to Have on Hand:

   salt, pepper, celery salt, olive oil, red wine vinegar, Dijon mustard, chicken stock (see page 276), superfine sugar, confectioner's sugar, almond extract, Burgundy

THE WORK SCHEDULE

4 Days Before Serving

1. Check the staples on hand and make your shopping list.
2. Buy everything you will need with the exception of the mushrooms, meats, eggs, heavy cream, and cottage cheese.
3. Prepare the meringues (through step 4 of the recipe), wrap, and freeze. They need little time to defrost.

3 Days Before Serving

1. Buy the eggs, heavy cream, and cottage cheese.
2. Order the meats for the pâté.
3. Prepare the Cream of Celery Soup, cover, and refrigerate. (Double the recipe when possible and freeze half for another day.)

2 Days Before Serving

1. Pick up the meats for the pâté.
2. Prepare the pâté completely. Cool thoroughly, wrap securely, and refrigerate.

1 Day Before Serving

1. Buy the mushrooms.
2. Prepare and cook the vegetables for the salad through step 5 of the recipe. Dry and store in the refrigerator in plastic bags.
3. Make the Vinaigrette Dressing for the salad (see page 282), place in a screw-top jar, and refrigerate.
4. If you are serving the soup cold, chill the soup bowls.
5. Set the table and select the wine.

Serving Day

1. *Two hours before serving,* remove the pâté from the refrigerator and let it come to room temperature.
2. *One hour before serving,* assemble the salad (steps 6 and 7 of the recipe) and refrigerate until needed.
3. *One hour before serving,* whip the cream and assemble the torte with the filling (steps 5 and 6 of the recipe), and refrigerate until needed.
4. Prepare the coffee maker and uncork the wine and decant it if necessary.

CREAM OF CELERY SOUP

1 head celery	Pepper
1 knob celeriac, or 2 small potatoes	Celery salt
4 cups chicken stock (see page 276)	Finely chopped parsley
1 medium onion, diced	

1. Remove the strings from the celery stalks with a vegetable peeler. Chop the stalks coarsely.

2. Wash, peel, and slice the celeriac or potatoes.

3. Put the vegetables and stock into a 2-quart saucepan with a tight-fitting lid. Bring to a boil, reduce the heat, and simmer covered for 15 minutes, or until tender.

4. Strain into a clean pan and purée the vegetables with some of the liquid in a food processor or blender, or put through a food mill. Stir the purée into the liquid and season with pepper and celery salt to taste. (Go easy on the pepper.) Serve hot or cold, garnished with parsley.

⇓ ⇓ ⇓

PÂTÉ DE VIANDE

2 pounds ground top round or sirloin	½ cup bottled chili sauce
1 pound ground veal	3 eggs, beaten
1 pound ground pork	3 tablespoons chopped green pepper
1 cup cottage cheese	Salt and pepper
1 cup fresh bread crumbs	½ cup Burgundy
1 cup chopped onion	1 cup tomato sauce

1. Preheat the oven to 400°F.

2. Combine the beef, veal, and pork and mix thoroughly. Add the cottage cheese, bread crumbs, onion, chili sauce, eggs, and green pepper. Season with salt and pepper to taste. Shape into a loaf and put into a roasting pan.

3. Pour the wine over the meat loaf and spread the tomato sauce over the loaf. Bake for 30 minutes, basting frequently. Reduce the oven temperature to 350°F. and bake for 1 hour, or until done. Baste frequently as the loaf bakes. Refrigerate and serve cold.

VEGETABLE SALAD

10 ounces green beans
4 carrots
3 celery stalks
½ small head cauliflower
4 cups water
1 teaspoon salt
¼ pound mushrooms
3 tablespoons chopped parsley
Vinaigrette Dressing (see page 282)
Lettuce leaves

1. Wash the beans, top and tail them, and cut them in half on the bias.

2. Peel and scrape the carrots and slice thinly on the bias. Put the carrots into a bowl of cold water.

3. Wash the celery and shave off any tough fibers with a vegetable peeler. Slice on the bias.

4. Break up the cauliflower into bite-sized pieces and add to the cold water with the carrots.

5. Bring the water and salt to a boil. Add the carrots and celery and cook for 4 minutes. Remove with a slotted spoon and set aside. Add the cauliflower to the same water and cook at a rolling boil for 4 minutes. Remove with a slotted spoon and set aside. Add the green beans to the water, bring to a boil, and drain immediately.

6. Wipe the mushrooms with a clean damp cloth and slice them very thin.

7. In a bowl, combine all the drained vegetables with the mushrooms and parsley. Toss well with the Vinaigrette Dressing. Serve on lettuce leaves.

PECAN MERINGUE TORTE

4 egg whites
1 cup superfine sugar
¼ teaspoon vinegar
1 teaspoon almond extract
1 cup chopped pecans
1 cup heavy cream

1 cup raspberries or
　6 tablespoons apricot purée
Superfine sugar
Confectioner's sugar
Fresh strawberries dusted with sugar
　for garnish

1. Preheat the oven to 350° F.

2. Cover a baking sheet with parchment paper. Mark two 9-inch circles on the paper.

3. Beat the egg whites until stiff. Continue beating thoroughly until the egg whites are very stiff, adding the sugar gradually. Then add the vinegar and almond extract. Fold in the chopped nuts carefully.

4. Divide the meringue into two parts and spoon one part over each circle. Smooth with a damp spatula, but do not press down. Bake for 35 minutes. Turn off the heat and allow the meringue to cool in the oven.

5. Whip the heavy cream until spoonfuls hold their shape. Stir in the raspberries or the apricot purée. Sweeten to taste. I suggest 3 tablespoons of superfine sugar.

6. Spread the filling over 1 meringue circle and place the other on top. Dust with confectioner's sugar. Garnish with fresh strawberries dusted with sugar.

⇟ ⇟ ⇟

THE MENU

Smoked Haddock Muscatel in Aspic
Langue de Boeuf Fumée with Cranberry-Cumberland Sauce
Baked Apples

A menu of smoked haddock and green grapes—preferably muscatels—smoked tongue, and baked apples is taking the diner from an exotic fish to a much misunderstood meat and then asking him to appreciate a mundane fruit for dessert. It is a culinary seesaw, but one that won't disappoint the palate. Choose the grapes and apples carefully: Look for a sharp flavor in both and a hardness in the apple.

THE INGREDIENTS

What You Will Need:

2 celery stalks

2 carrots

1 small onion

1 bunch watercress

White seedless grapes

6 large Granny Smith or Greening apples

6 lemons

2 oranges

2 cups fresh strawberries

8 ounces smoked haddock

5- to 6-pound smoked beef tongue

1 large egg

2 tablespoons unsalted butter

1 pint heavy cream

Milk

1 tablespoon unflavored gelatin

½ cup red currant jelly

Staples to Have on Hand:

salt, pepper, peppercorns, ground nutmeg, cinnamon sticks, whole allspice, bay leaf; fish, chicken, or veal stock; granulated sugar, light port wine

THE WORK SCHEDULE

3 Days Before Serving
1. Check the staples on hand and make your shopping list.
2. Buy everything you will need.

2 Days Before Serving
1. Cook the tongue; when cool enough to handle, skin it and remove the bone, fat, and gristle from the thick end. Reserve the liquid the tongue was cooked in. Squeeze the tongue into a small round saucepan or bowl so that it is coiled. Chill the cooking liquid, remove the fat, and pour enough of the liquid over the coiled tongue to cover it. Cover securely. Refrigerate the remaining liquid and the tongue separately.
2. Prepare the fish for the first course (through step 1 of the recipe), but do not flake it. Reserve ¼ cup of the poaching liquid. Cover and refrigerate fish and liquid separately.
3. Prepare the Cranberry-Cumberland Sauce, cool, cover, and refrigerate.

1 Day Before Serving
1. Prepare the fish purée and the aspic and complete the Smoked Haddock dish through step 6 of the recipe. Cover and refrigerate.
2. Core the baking apples and fill them (steps 1 through 4 of the recipe). Cover and refrigerate.
3. Slice the tongue and arrange it in an ovenproof dish for heating. Spoon some of the tongue liquid over it. Cover and return to the refrigerator.
4. Set the table and select the wine.

Serving Day
1. Bake the apples early in the day, selecting the time that suits you best. If you want to serve them warm, you can reheat them while you are serving the main course.
2. *Two hours before serving*, unmold the first course (step 7 of the recipe) and refrigerate until needed.
3. *One half-hour before serving*, reheat the tongue and pour the Cranberry-Cumberland Sauce into a sauceboat.
4. Whip the cream for the Baked Apples and refrigerate until needed.
5. Prepare the coffee maker and uncork the wine.

SMOKED HADDOCK MUSCATEL

8 ounces smoked haddock
Equal amounts of milk and water to
  cover the fish
¼ cup reserved poaching liquid from
  the fish
1 cup aspic (see following recipe)

Grated peel of 1 lemon
Salt, pepper, and ground nutmeg
¾ cup heavy cream
White seedless grapes
Watercress sprigs for garnish

1. Cover the fish with the milk and water mixture and bring slowly to a boil (the mixture boils over easily and makes an incredible mess if not watched), reduce the heat, and simmer for 1 or 2 minutes. Drain the fish and flake it.

2. Put the flaked fish and ¼ cup of the poaching liquid into a food processor or blender and purée. Scrape the purée into a clean bowl and stir in ¼ cup liquid aspic and the lemon peel. Season with salt, pepper, and nutmeg to taste. Chill.

3. Beat the cream until soft peaks are formed and fold the beaten cream into the chilled fish purée.

4. Spoon 1 tablespoon of aspic into six ½-cup molds and allow to set.

5. Arrange enough grapes on the aspic to cover it. Add about 2 tablespoons of aspic to the molds to cover the grapes. Chill the molds to set the aspic.

6. Fill the molds with the fish purée and chill for at least 2 hours before unmolding.

7. To unmold, wring out a towel which has been soaked in hot water and wrap it around each mold. Turn the molds out on a serving platter and garnish with watercress.

QUICK ASPIC

1½ cups cold fish, chicken, or veal stock (see stock chapter, pages 276-77)
1 small onion, thinly sliced

1 eggshell, crushed
1 egg white, lightly beaten
1 tablespoon unflavored gelatin

1. Combine the stock, onion, eggshell, and egg white in a saucepan. Simmer for 10 minutes. Do not allow the mixture to boil. Cool for 20 minutes.

2. Strain the mixture through 3 or 4 thicknesses of cheesecloth to clarify.

3. Soften the gelatin by sprinkling it over ½ cup of the strained stock. Dissolve the gelatin over very low heat and add to the clarified stock. Cool before using.

↯ ↯ ↯

LANGUE DE BOEUF FUMÉE

2 celery stalks, chopped
2 carrots, chopped
1 bay leaf
3 tablespoons salt
8 peppercorns

1 5- to 6-pound smoked beef tongue
Cranberry-Cumberland Sauce (see page 281)

1. Put the celery, carrots, bay leaf, salt, peppercorns, and tongue in a pot large enough to hold the tongue. Add sufficient cold water to cover by 1 inch. Bring to a boil, reduce the heat, cover and simmer for 2½ hours.

2. Turn off the heat and leave the tongue in the stock until you are ready to skin and dress it.

3. To serve, remove the tongue from the stock and skin it. The skin comes off easily. Remove the bones, cartilage, and fat from the thick end of the tongue.

4. Carve horizontally from the thin end. To keep the tongue moist, spoon a little of the stock over the tongue. Serve with Cranberry-Cumberland Sauce.

BAKED APPLES

6 large hard Granny Smith or Greening apples
2 tablespoons unsalted butter

6 tablespoons granulated sugar
½ cup lemon juice
Whipped cream for garnish

1. Preheat the oven to 375°F.

2. Core the apples and run a small sharp knife around each apple at its widest point.

3. Mix together the butter, sugar, and 1 tablespoon of lemon juice. Fill the holes in the apples with this mixture.

4. Arrange the apples in a shallow ovenproof dish with a cover. Sprinkle the apples with the remaining lemon juice.

5. Cover and bake for 25 minutes. Uncover and baste with the pan juices. Bake until the apples are tender. Serve hot or at room temperature with the whipped cream.

⇓ ⇓ ⇓

THE MENU

Mushrooms à la Grecque
Butterflied Leg of Lamb
Salad Bagatelle
Paris Brest

Mushrooms à la Grecque, lean broiled lamb, a salad of vegetables lightly dressed with a simple vinaigrette, followed by a wickedly rich Paris Brest is a splendid repast varied in texture, color, and flavor. In spite of the dessert, the meal is not high in calories (provided you don't go overboard on the last course).

The chou paste ring for the dessert freezes well (without the filling), provided it is wrapped and sealed. Make two and freeze one for another day! The leg of lamb when skillfully boned yields more servings than one cooked with the bone intact. It is much easier to carve for those who are not experts in the art; and, lastly, it allows for a range of doneness—from well done to pale pink—to accommodate a variety of tastes.

THE INGREDIENTS

What You Will Need:

2 pounds medium mushrooms
½ pound asparagus
4 medium carrots
2 celery stalks
4 shallots
1 ripe tomato
1 bunch parsley
6 lemons

2 heads Boston lettuce
5-pound leg of lamb, butterflied
1 dozen large eggs
½ pint heavy cream
¾ pound unsalted butter
½ cup slivered almonds
½ cup blanched almonds

Staples to Have on Hand:

 salt, pepper, Dijon mustard, cream of tartar, soy sauce, garlic cloves, tomato paste, olive oil, red wine vinegar, granulated sugar, dark brown sugar, flour

THE WORK SCHEDULE

3 Days Before Serving
1. Check the staples on hand and make your shopping list.
2. Buy everything you will need with the exception of the mushrooms.
3. Order the lamb.
4. Make the sauce for the lamb (step 1 of the recipe), cover, and refrigerate.

2 Days Before Serving
1. Make the Vinaigrette Dressing (see page 282) and refrigerate in a jar.
2. Prepare the Praline Powder (see page 135) and refrigerate in a screw-top jar. It keeps indefinitely.
3. Prepare and blanch the vegetables for the Salad Bagatelle (steps 1 and 2 of the recipe). Dry thoroughly, put into plastic bags, and refrigerate.

1 Day Before Serving
1. Buy the mushrooms.
2. If your butcher has not already boned the lamb, bone it now. Cook the lamb, cool, wrap securely, and refrigerate.
3. Prepare the pastry for the Paris Brest (through step 5 of the recipe). Cool, wrap securely, and refrigerate.
4. Prepare the Crème Pralinée for the Paris Brest, cover, and refrigerate.
5. Prepare the Mushrooms à la Grecque (through step 4 of the recipe), cover, and refrigerate.
6. Set the table and select the wine.

Serving Day
1. *Late in the afternoon,* whip the cream, split the pastry, and assemble the Paris Brest (steps 6 and 7 of the recipe). Refrigerate until ready to serve.
2. *Two hours before serving,* remove lamb from refrigerator to allow it to come to room temperature.
3. *One hour before serving,* slice the mushrooms for the Salad Bagatelle and mix them raw with the blanched vegetables in a bowl ready for dressing with the vinaigrette.
4. *One hour before serving,* take the Mushrooms à la Grecque out of the refrigerator and arrange on a serving platter.
5. Prepare the coffee maker and uncork the wine.

131

MUSHROOMS À LA GRECQUE

1½ pounds medium mushrooms
4 shallots, chopped
2 tablespoons olive oil
2 tablespoons unsalted butter
1 small clove garlic, crushed with 1
  teaspoon salt
½ tablespoon salt

2 heaping tablespoons tomato paste
1 ripe tomato, peeled, seeded, and
  chopped
Lemon juice
½ cup parsley sprigs, finely chopped
Lettuce leaves

1. Wipe the mushrooms with a clean damp cloth. Cut the stems off flush with the caps and quarter the caps. (Reserve the stems for use in another dish.)

2. Sauté the shallots in the oil and butter but do not let them brown. Add the crushed garlic and mushrooms. Cook, turning often, for 5 minutes. Add the salt and cook until the mushrooms give up their juices.

3. Stir in the tomato paste and tomato. Cook, stirring, for a few minutes longer.

4. Pour the mixture into a bowl and cool. Correct the seasonings and add the lemon juice to taste and the parsley.

5. Serve on lettuce leaves at room temperature.

⌄⌄⌄

BUTTERFLIED LEG OF LAMB

⅓ cup lemon juice
4 tablespoons dark brown sugar
1 clove garlic, crushed with salt
2 tablespoons Dijon mustard
2 tablespoons soy sauce

½ teaspoon salt
¼ teaspoon pepper
2 tablespoons olive oil
1 5-pound leg of lamb, butterflied
  and flattened

1. In a small bowl, mix together the lemon juice, brown sugar, garlic, mustard, soy sauce, salt, and pepper. Gradually add the oil.

2. One hour before cooking, brush the lamb with the sauce.

3. Preheat the oven to 475°F.

4. Put the lamb on a wire rack in a roasting pan. Roast on the highest shelf of the oven for 10 minutes on each side, brushing frequently with the sauce.

5. Remove from the oven. Cool, cover, and refrigerate. Serve at room temperature, sliced thinly and on the bias, as you would a London broil.

⇓⇓⇓

SALAD BAGATELLE

½ pound fresh asparagus
Salt
4 medium carrots, julienned
2 celery stalks, julienned

½ pound mushrooms, sliced
½ cup parsley sprigs, chopped
Vinaigrette Dressing (see page 282)
1 head Boston lettuce

1. Remove the outer peel of the asparagus and slice on the bias into 1-inch slices.

2. Bring a pan of water to boil and add 1 tablespoon salt for every quart of water. Add the julienned carrots and bring to a boil. Lift out the carrots immediately. Blanch the celery and asparagus in this same manner, taking extra care to see that they are not overcooked. The vegetables must be crisp.

3. Toss the blanched vegetables, raw mushrooms, and parsley with the vinaigrette, using just enough to coat them liberally. Serve on lettuce leaves.

⇓⇓⇓

PARIS BREST

1 cup water
4 tablespoons unsalted butter
Pinch of salt
1 cup flour
4 eggs

1 egg beaten with 1 tablespoon water
½ cup slivered almonds
Crème Pralinée (see following recipe)
1 cup heavy cream

1. Preheat the oven to 400°F.

2. Lightly butter and flour a baking sheet. Shake off any excess flour. Trace an 8-inch circle in the center of the baking sheet.

3. Put the water, butter, and salt in a heavy saucepan and heat until the butter has melted. Bring to a rolling boil and add the flour all at once. Remove from the heat and stir until the mixture leaves the sides and bottom of the pan. Transfer to a clean mixing bowl, cool slightly, and stir in the eggs one at a time, beating well after each addition.

4. Fill a pastry bag fitted with a large plain nozzle with the chou paste. Squeeze out a ring of the paste about 1 inch high and 2 inches thick inside the circle marked on the baking sheet. Brush with the beaten egg and scatter the almonds on top.

5. Bake for 40 minutes. Turn off the oven and allow the pastry ring to cool in the oven with the door ajar.

6. Split the pastry ring. Fill the bottom half with the Crème Pralinée. Fill the dents in the upper half with the cream also.

7. Whip the heavy cream until stiff. Pile on the bottom half of the pastry ring and cover with the top half.

CRÈME PRALINÉE

9 tablespoons granulated sugar
¼ cup water
⅛ teaspoon cream of tartar
5 egg yolks, beaten

1 cup unsalted butter, softened
¼ cup Praline Powder (see following
  recipe)

1. Stir the sugar, water, and cream of tartar over low heat until the sugar is dissolved. Raise the heat and cook the syrup rapidly without stirring until it spins a thread (240°F. on a candy thermometer).

2. Beat the syrup gradually into the beaten egg yolks. Continue to beat until the cream is thick and cool.

3. Beat the softened butter gradually into the cream and stir in the Praline Powder.

PRALINE POWDER

¾ cup granulated sugar
¼ cup water

¼ teaspoon cream of tartar
½ cup blanched almonds

1. Put all the ingredients in a heavy saucepan. Heat and stir until the sugar dissolves. Continue to heat without stirring until a dark amber color.

2. Pour onto a lightly buttered cookie sheet and cool.

3. Break into rough pieces and pulverize in a blender or food processor. Store in a screw-top jar in the refrigerator.

⅄ ⅄ ⅄

THE MENU

Coquilles St. Jacques
Shepherd's Pie
Valerie's Cold Orange Soufflé

Two beautiful classics and a dish considered to be family fare too commonplace for guests make up this menu.

Coquilles St. Jacques gets its title from pilgrims to the monastery at Santiago de Compostela in Spain. To show that they had made the pilgrimage to honor St. James, they wore scallop shells in their hats.

It is customary to serve the coquilles in individual scallop shells, but I've found that when the shells go under the broiler, they tend to crack. And besides, not everyone has the shells. If an ovenproof dish is used, there is no risk, and it makes a more spectacular presentation.

Shepherd's Pie, simple as it is, when suitably garnished is a dish fit for a king. When I was involved in catering, time after time I talked a hostess into serving it at a formal buffet. It was always a resounding success.

The dessert is another tour de force. And well it should be, for it has been put to the test in that glamorous watering hole, Palm Beach. Valerie Johnson has graciously given me permission to use her recipe.

THE INGREDIENTS

What You Will Need:

2 medium onions

2 or 3 shallots

½ pound small white mushrooms

1 bunch parsley sprigs

1 pound potatoes

4 oranges

1 lemon (optional)

2 pounds scallops

3 pounds lean lamb, ground

½ dozen large eggs

¼ pound unsalted butter

1½ pints heavy cream

Bread crumbs

1 envelope unflavored gelatin

Dry white wine

Staples to Have on Hand:

salt, pepper, dried rosemary, chicken stock (see page 276) optional, granulated sugar, flour

⇊ ⇊ ⇊

THE WORK SCHEDULE

2 Days Before Serving

1. Check the staples on hand and make your shopping list.
2. Buy everything you will need.

1 Day Before Serving

1. Prepare the Shepherd's Pie (through step 1 of the recipe) and spoon it into its serving dish, but do not add the potato topping. Cover and refrigerate.
2. Prepare the Coquilles St. Jacques (through step 5 of the recipe). Cover and refrigerate.
3. Prepare Valerie's Soufflé (through step 5 of the recipe). Cover and chill. Do not garnish until Serving Day, because orange segments are inclined to weep.
4. Set the table and select the wine.

Serving Day

1. Boil the potatoes for the Shepherd's Pie.
2. Take the Shepherd's Pie and the Coquilles St. Jacques out of the refrigerator early in the day to give them time to reach room temperature. Top the Shepherd's Pie with the riced potatoes.
3. *One half-hour before serving,* preheat the oven to 350°F. to reheat both the coquilles (step 6) and the pie (step 3). Run the first course under the broiler just before serving. Both dishes should be garnished with chopped parsley just before serving.
4. *One half-hour before serving,* garnish the soufflé with the whipped cream and orange segments. Return the soufflé to the refrigerator.
5. Prepare the coffee maker and uncork the wine.

⅄ ⅄ ⅄

COQUILLES ST. JACQUES

2 pounds scallops
2 cups dry white wine
4 tablespoons unsalted butter
2 to 3 shallots, chopped fine
½ pound small white mushrooms,
 thinly sliced

3 tablespoons flour
¾ cup heavy cream
Salt, pepper, and lemon juice
Buttered bread crumbs
Finely chopped parsley

1. Bring the scallops to a boil in the wine and drain right away, setting aside the liquid and any more that seeps from the scallops.

2. Melt 3 tablespoons butter in a heavy pan and sauté the shallots until they are soft. Add the sliced mushrooms and cook for 3 to 4 minutes, or until the mushrooms have given up their moisture. Sprinkle with the flour and mix in well.

3. Add the reserved scallop liquid and stir until smooth. Cook slowly for 7 to 8 minutes to reduce.

4. Stir in the cream and continue reducing until the sauce is thick—rather like extra-heavy cream. Season with salt and pepper to taste and a little lemon juice, if you like (it won't do any harm).

5. Add the scallops to the sauce and spoon the mixture into individual buttered scallop shells or ovenproof dishes. Cover and refrigerate.

6. To serve, sprinkle lightly with buttered bread crumbs and reheat in a 350°F. oven. Brown under the broiler if necessary. Sprinkle with the chopped parsley just before serving.

↯ ↯ ↯

SHEPHERD'S PIE

2 medium onions, peeled and chopped
3 tablespoons butter
3 pounds lean lamb, put once through the meat grinder
Pinch of dried rosemary

Salt and pepper
3 or 4 potatoes, about 1 pound, peeled and boiled
Chicken stock to moisten, if needed
Finely chopped parsley

1. Sauté the onions in the butter until they are golden. Stir in the ground lamb and rosemary. Cook, stirring, for 3 to 4 minutes. (If overcooked, the dish becomes dry and grainy.) Season with salt and pepper to taste. Moisten with chicken stock if too dry. Turn into a flat ovenproof dish not more than 2 inches deep. Cool, cover, and refrigerate.

2. Using a ricer, cover the lamb with the boiled potatoes. Do not pat the potatoes down but leave them light and airy and completely covering the lamb.

3. Preheat the oven to 350°F. Bake for 20 minutes, then run under the broiler for 1 minute to color the potato topping a healthy brown. Sprinkle with chopped parsley and serve.

VALERIE'S COLD ORANGE SOUFFLÉ

3 eggs, separated
½ cup granulated sugar
Grated peel of 3 oranges, about 2
   tablespoons

1 cup fresh orange juice
1 envelope unflavored gelatin
2 cups heavy cream
Orange segments for garnish

1. Beat the egg yolks and sugar with an electric mixer at medium speed for 5 minutes. Or beat with a whisk for 10 minutes by hand. Stir in the grated orange peel and ¾ cup orange juice.

2. Soften the gelatin in the remaining orange juice and heat over hot water until thoroughly liquefied. Cool and beat into the egg mixture.

3. Whip the egg whites until very stiff.

4. Whip 1⅓ cups heavy cream until stiff, but do not overbeat. Fold the egg whites and whipped cream into the egg mixture.

5. Transfer the soufflé to a glass serving dish (or a soufflé dish), cover, and chill thoroughly.

6. At serving time, or a little before, whip the remaining cream. With a pastry tube, decorate the top of the soufflé with a swirl pattern and arrange the orange segments as you wish. Refrigerate until serving time.

↡↡↡

THE MENU

Cold Cucumber Soup
Moussaka
Pear and Strawberry Compote

Cold Cucumber Soup acts as an apéritif: Tangy, it prepares the palate for the richness of the Moussaka to follow. In one of my recent classes a student complained that a plate of Moussaka without garnish looked naked. I suggested baking extra slices of eggplant and using them as garnish. If tomatoes are home-grown, a few slices, brushed with oil and baked, could be added for color.

The compote that follows is cool on the tongue and enticing to the eye.

THE INGREDIENTS

What You Will Need:

4 medium cucumbers
4 medium onions
1 red onion
2 medium eggplants
2 lemons
1 bunch parsley
1 bunch fresh dill
8 not-too-ripe pears

2 pints strawberries
4 pounds lean lamb, ground once
½ pound unsalted butter
½ pint sour cream
Milk
¾ cup grated Romano cheese
2 8-ounce cans tomato sauce

Staples to Have on Hand:

  salt, coarse salt, pepper, peppercorns, bay leaf, ground nutmeg, dried thyme, cinnamon sticks, whole cloves, olive oil, chicken stock (see page 276), flour, granulated sugar

THE WORK SCHEDULE

3 Days Before Serving

1. Check the staples on hand and make your shopping list.
2. Buy everything you will need with the exception of the dill, parsley, and strawberries.
3. Order the lamb.

2 Days Before Serving

1. Pick up the lamb.
2. Poach the pears (through step 2 of the recipe). Cool, cover, and refrigerate.
3. Prepare the eggplant for the Moussaka (step 1 of the recipe). Cover and refrigerate.

1 Day Before Serving

1. Buy the dill, parsley, and strawberries. Wash the strawberries, dry, and refrigerate.
2. Prepare the Béchamel Sauce (see page 278) and the Moussaka through step 6 of the recipe. Cool, cover, and refrigerate.
3. Prepare the soup (through step 3 of the recipe), cover, and refrigerate.
4. Chill the bowls for the soup.
5. Set the table and select the wine.

Serving Day

1. *Two hours before serving*, take the Moussaka out of the refrigerator.
2. *One hour before serving*, add the strawberries to the pears in a serving dish. If the strawberries are large, halve or quarter them. Refrigerate until needed.
3. *Forty-five minutes before serving*, preheat the oven to 350°F. and heat the Moussaka for 30 minutes.
4. Prepare the coffee maker and uncork the wine.

⇊ ⇊ ⇊

COLD CUCUMBER SOUP

4 medium cucumbers
4 cups chicken stock (see page 276)
1 red onion, peeled and chopped
1 cup sour cream (optional)

Salt, pepper, and lemon juice
3 to 4 tablespoons snipped fresh dill
2 tablespoons finely chopped parsley

1. Wash, peel, and remove the seeds from 2 cucumbers. Dice the cucumbers.

2. Put 1 cup of stock, the diced cucumbers, and the onion into a heavy pan and simmer until tender. Purée in a blender until smooth. Pour into a bowl and add the remaining stock.

3. Peel and remove the seeds of the remaining cucumbers. Grate coarsely and stir into the soup with the sour cream. Season the soup with salt, pepper, and lemon juice to taste. Stir in the snipped dill and chill thoroughly.

4. Serve cold in cold bowls, sprinkled with the parsley.

↯ ↯ ↯

MOUSSAKA

2 medium eggplants
Coarse salt
Olive oil
1 stick (4 ounces) unsalted butter
4 medium onions, sliced
4 pounds lean lamb, ground once
1 teaspoon ground nutmeg
1 teaspoon dried thyme

2 8-ounce cans tomato sauce
Salt and pepper
½ cup parsley sprigs, chopped
4 cups Béchamel Sauce (see page 278)
   seasoned with a pinch of nutmeg
   and ½ cup grated Romano cheese
¼ cup grated Romano cheese

1. Remove only three or four narrow strips of skin from each eggplant, paring from tip to tail. Slice the eggplant horizontally into ¼-inch-thick slices. Arrange the slices in one layer on baking sheets. Sprinkle the slices with coarse salt. Cover with additional baking sheets and weight them down. Let sit for 2 to 3 hours, or overnight in the refrigerator.

2. Preheat the oven to 350°F.

(Continued)

145

3. Pour off any liquid around the eggplant slices and dry the slices with paper towels. Arrange the slices in a single layer on well-oiled jelly roll pans. Bake for 10 to 15 minutes, or until tender.

4. Melt the butter in a large skillet and cook the onions until soft and lightly browned. Add the ground lamb, nutmeg, and thyme. Stir to mix well and cook, stirring, for 3 to 4 minutes. Add the tomato sauce and mix well. Cover and cook over low heat for 15 to 20 minutes, stirring occasionally. Season with salt and pepper to taste and stir in the parsley.

5. Preheat the oven to 350°F.

6. Arrange the eggplant slices on the bottom of a 9 × 14 × 1½-inch ovenproof dish. Cover with the cooked lamb and top with more eggplant slices. Spoon the Béchamel Sauce evenly over the top layer of eggplant. Sprinkle with the cheese. Bake in the top half of the oven for 25 to 30 minutes, or until lightly browned.

☇ ☇ ☇

PEAR AND STRAWBERRY COMPOTE

8 cups water
3 cups granulated sugar
4 cinnamon sticks
8 whole cloves

1 lemon, cut into quarters
8 not-too-ripe pears
2 pints strawberries

1. Combine the water and sugar in a saucepan with a lid. Cook until the sugar is dissolved. Add the cinnamon, cloves, and lemon quarters, cover, and simmer for ½ hour.

2. Peel the pears, cut them in half, and carefully remove the cores. Simmer gently in the poaching syrup until they test soft when pierced with a toothpick. (The poaching time will vary with the degree of ripeness of the pears.) Cool the pears in the syrup.

3. Wash, hull, and drain the strawberries.

4. Mix the strawberries with the cooled pears and 2 cups of the poaching syrup. Chill.

⇟ ⇟ ⇟

THE MENU

Coleslaw
Cassoulet
Compote of Pears and Grapes

Cassoulet is native to southwest France, and each district has its own method and recipe for this hearty dish. But all versions have one ingredient in common—the small white bean. Many cooks are under the impression that preserved goose is essential. I have found that a reasonably good simulation is reached with pork and sausage. Cassoulet is so hearty that in my opinion it should be served at midday and not in the evening.

A green salad is all that should accompany the entrée, with fresh fruit to follow. In this case, coleslaw as a first course is sufficiently light that it will not dull the palate, and a simple fruit compote takes the place of fresh fruit.

A wine that would enhance this dish is the Onion Skin, a rosé from the region west of Marseilles.

THE INGREDIENTS

What You Will Need:

½ head cabbage
2 carrots
1 small green pepper
1 large onion
2 celery stalks with leaves
Lettuce
2 lemons
1 bunch parsley
8 Bartlett, Comice, or Anjou pears

1 pound seedless grapes
1½ pounds boneless pork loin in one
   piece
¼ pound fresh or salt pork rind
1 pound pork sausage
1½ pounds small Great Northern
   beans
Large eggs
Sour cream

Staples to Have on Hand:

   salt, celery salt, pepper, dried thyme, bay leaf, garlic cloves, Dijon mustard,
Tabasco, olive oil, red wine vinegar, cinnamon sticks, whole cloves, granulated
sugar

THE WORK SCHEDULE

3 Days Before Serving
1. Check the staples on hand and make your shopping list.
2. Buy everything you will need with the exception of the pork loin, pork rind, and sausage.

2 Days Before Serving
1. Buy the pork loin, pork rind, and sausage, and refrigerate.
2. Blanch the pork rind (step 4 of the recipe), drain, cover, and refrigerate.
3. Roast the pork loin (steps 2 and 3 of recipe). Cool, cover, and refrigerate.
4. Soak the beans for the Cassoulet overnight (step 1 of the recipe).
5. Prepare the vegetables and dressing for the Coleslaw. Cover and store separately in the refrigerator.

1 Day Before Serving
1. Finish cooking the Cassoulet (steps 5 through 8), allowing at least 4 hours for this. Cool and refrigerate.
2. Poach the pears for the compote. Remove the seeds from the grapes if they are not seedless, and assemble the compote and refrigerate.
3. Set the table and select the wines.

Serving Day
1. *One hour before serving*, assemble the Coleslaw and refrigerate.
2. *Forty-five minutes before serving*, preheat the oven to 350°F. and reheat the Cassoulet. Sprinkle with parsley before serving.
3. Serve the compote directly from the refrigerator.
4. Prepare the coffee maker and uncork the wines.

⚜ ⚜ ⚜

COLESLAW

¼ cup mayonnaise (see page 280)
⅓ cup sour cream
¼ teaspoon lemon juice
1 tablespoon red wine vinegar
1 tablespoon Dijon mustard
Salt and pepper
Dash of Tabasco

Pinch of celery salt
½ head cabbage, sliced thin
2 carrots, shredded
½ green pepper, seeded, sliced thin, and diced
¼ cup parsley sprigs, chopped
Lettuce leaves

1. Combine the mayonnaise, sour cream, lemon juice, vinegar, mustard, salt and pepper to taste, Tabasco, and celery salt and mix well.

3. Mix the cabbage, carrots, green pepper, and parsley in a bowl. Stir the dressing into the vegetables a little at a time so as not to make them too wet. Serve on lettuce leaves.

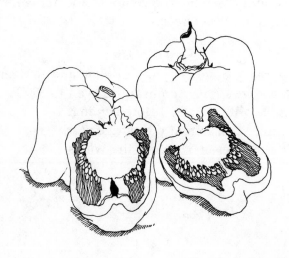

CASSOULET

1½ pounds small Great Northern beans
Salt
1½ pounds boneless pork loin in one piece
¼ pound fresh or salt pork rind
1 large onion, sliced

2 celery stalks with leaves, chopped
1 bay leaf
Large pinch of dried thyme
2 cloves garlic
1 pound pork sausage
Pepper
1 cup parsley sprigs, chopped

1. Soak the beans overnight in cold water to cover. Add 1 tablespoon salt to the soaking water.

2. Preheat the oven to 325°F.

3. Remove all fat from the pork. Put the pork in a roasting pan and roast until the internal temperature is approximately 275°F. Set aside to cool. Reserve the pan juices.

4. Blanch the pork rind by covering it with cold water and bringing the water to a boil. Drain and repeat the process three more times. Drain for the last time and cut the rind into neat triangles.

5. The next day, preheat the oven to 325°F.

6. Drain the beans and transfer them to a large clay pot. Cover with fresh water and add the onion, celery, bay leaf, thyme, garlic, and blanched pork rind. Cover and bake for 4 hours.

7. Slice the sausage and cut the pork loin into 1-inch cubes. After the beans have cooked for 3 hours, add the sliced sausage, pork cubes, and the reserved pan juices. Stir to mix well and season with salt and pepper to taste.

8. Return the uncovered pot to the oven. Bake for ½ hour, or until a brown crust forms on top. Stir the crust gently into the bean mixture. Bake again until a second crust forms. (The crust may be encouraged by sprinkling the top with a layer of fresh white bread crumbs.)

9. To serve, sprinkle each serving with parsley.

COMPOTE OF PEARS AND GRAPES

1 cup granulated sugar
4 cups water
Juice of 1 lemon
2 cinnamon sticks

4 whole cloves
8 Bartlett, Comice, or Anjou pears
1 pound seedless grapes

1. Dissolve the sugar in the water in a saucepan with a tight-fitting lid. Add the lemon juice and spices and simmer for 10 to 15 minutes.

2. Peel and core the pears. Halve or quarter them according to your taste.

3. Put the pears carefully into the boiling syrup and poach until they test tender when pierced with a toothpick. Allow the pears to cool in the syrup. Cover and refrigerate.

4. Wash and halve the grapes. Drain the pears and mix with the grapes. Serve in a glass dish with a little of the poaching syrup.

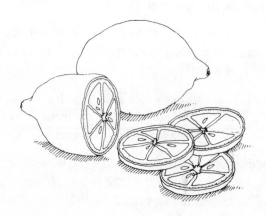

⇟⇟⇟

THE MENU

Salad San Diego
Saucisson en Brioche with Sauce Madeira
Strawberries Escoffier

Don't be put off by the apparent complexity of this menu's entrée. Study the steps carefully and you will find simplicity in the method. The Brown Sauce, once it has been put together and left to simmer over low heat, needs no further attention. When it has been sufficiently reduced, strained, and cooled, the sauce may be refrigerated for 3 or 4 days or frozen for a month or two. To create a Sauce Madeira, all that you need to do is stir in the correct amount of Madeira after the Brown Sauce has been heated.

The preparation of brioche is a leisurely one that leaves ample time to relax between steps. It is a simple dough to handle, as it rolls out smoothly and can be wrapped around the sausage like a well-fitting glove.

The first and last courses are simply a matter of following the directions. The completed menu gives contrast in flavor, color, and texture.

THE INGREDIENTS

What You Will Need:

1 carrot
1 small onion
1 celery stalk
2 pounds asparagus
6 to 8 radishes
1 not-too-ripe avocado
1 large bunch parsley
Lettuce
2 pints strawberries

2 oranges
1 lemon
¼ pound lean bacon
1½- to 2-pound garlic sausage
¼ pound unsalted butter
3 large eggs
1 pint heavy cream
1 pint milk
1 package dry yeast

Staples to Have on Hand:

   salt, pepper, peppercorns, bay leaf, Dijon mustard, red wine vinegar, olive oil, beef stock, tomato paste, flour, granulated sugar, Grand Marnier

THE WORK SCHEDULE

3 Days Before Serving

1. Check the staples on hand and make your shopping list.
2. Buy the sausage for the Saucisson. Cook (steps 5 and 6 of the recipe), cool, wrap tightly, and refrigerate.
3. Buy the ingredients for the Brown Sauce (see page 277) and start it simmering. Strain the sauce when done; cool, cover, and refrigerate.

2 Days Before Serving

1. Prepare the brioche for the Saucisson (steps 1 through 4 of the recipe); and when it has risen, punch it down, cover, and refrigerate.
2. Buy the parsley, wash, dry, and refrigerate in a plastic bag.
3. Prepare the Vinaigrette Dressing (see page 282) and refrigerate in a screw-top jar.

1 Day Before Serving

1. Wrap the sausage in the brioche dough (steps 8 and 9 of the recipe), decorate, cover, and refrigerate.
2. Buy the asparagus, avocado, and radishes for the salad. Trim and cook the asparagus (steps 1 and 2 of the recipe). Slice the radishes (step 4 of the recipe). Refrigerate both in plastic bags.
3. Buy the strawberries, wash, hull, and dry. Refrigerate in a plastic bag.
4. Prepare the sauce for the strawberries (steps 2 through 4 of the recipe), cover, and refrigerate.
5. Set the table and select the wine.

Serving Day

1. *Two hours before baking time*, take the sausage in the brioche dough out of the refrigerator. Brush with the egg and water mixture just before baking. Don't discard the egg mixture—it may be necessary to brush the brioche halfway through the baking time if the color is not dark enough to please you.
2. *One hour before serving*, peel and cube the avocado and dress the San Diego Salad.
3. Stir the syrup into the strawberries, but do not refrigerate. Whip the cream and refrigerate.
4. *Forty-five minutes before serving*, preheat the oven to 375° F. and bake the Saucisson for 35 minutes (step 10 of the recipe).
5. Measure the Brown Sauce into a small pan ready for heating with the ¼ cup Madeira.
6. Arrange the salad on lettuce leaves. Sprinkle a little chopped parsley over each serving.
7. Prepare the coffee maker and uncork the wine.

SALAD SAN DIEGO

2 pounds asparagus
1 not-too-ripe avocado
Vinaigrette Dressing (see page 282)

6 to 8 radishes
Lettuce leaves
2 tablespoons finely chopped parsley

1. Scrape the asparagus stalks with a vegetable peeler and cut off the white ends if they are tough. Cut the asparagus on the bias into 1-inch pieces.

2. Drop the tips into boiling salted water and boil for 2 minutes. Remove and drain. Add the stalks and boil for 4 minutes. Remove and drain.

3. Peel the avocado and cut it into 2-inch cubes. Put the avocado cubes in a salad bowl and pour the Vinaigrette Dressing over them to prevent discoloration.

4. Trim the radishes and slice them very thinly. Cut the radish slices into julienne strips and add to the avocado. Add the cooled asparagus and toss lightly.

5. To serve, pile the mixture onto lettuce leaves and sprinkle with parsley.

SAUCISSON EN BRIOCHE

1 package dry yeast
2 tablespoons warm milk
1½ cups flour
1 teaspoon granulated sugar
½ teaspoon salt
2 eggs

1 stick (4 ounces) unsalted butter, softened
1 large (1½ to 2 pounds) garlic sausage (coteghini)
1 egg beaten with 1 tablespoon water
½ cup parsley sprigs, chopped
2 cups Madeira Sauce (see page 278)

1. Sprinkle the yeast over the milk to soften it.

2. In a bowl sift together the flour, sugar, and salt and make a well in the center. Put the 2 eggs into the well and add the softened yeast. Combine and knead all ingredients to make a smooth mixture.

3. With your hands, work in the butter until the dough is thoroughly mixed.

4. Shape the soft dough into a ball and put it in a bowl that has been sprinkled with flour. Cut a deep crosswise incision in the top of the dough. Cover the bowl with a towel and let the dough rise in a warm place with no drafts until it has doubled in size. Punch the dough down, cover again, and chill overnight.

5. Put the sausage in a pan in which it can lie flat. Cover the sausage with cold water and cook over low heat, with the water scarcely moving, for 45 to 60 minutes.

6. Remove the sausage from the water, cool, cover, and refrigerate.

7. Preheat the oven to 375°F.

8. Turn the brioche dough out onto a floured board and roll it into a rectangle about ¼ inch thick. Work swiftly while the dough is still firm from the chilling.

9. Skin the sausage and put it in the center of the dough. Gather the dough around it without stretching the dough. With fingers moistened in cold water, pinch the edges of the dough together lightly. If desired, press little cutouts of the dough on top. Put the roll on a lightly buttered baking sheet. Brush the top and sides with the egg and water mixture.

10. Bake for 35 minutes, or until the brioche is golden brown. Let the roll rest for about 5 minutes. Use a broad spatula to remove it carefully to a warm serving platter. Garnish with parsley and serve with Madeira Sauce in a warmed sauceboat. p. 278

⇓ ⇓ ⇓

STRAWBERRIES ESCOFFIER

2 pints strawberries
2 large oranges
4 tablespoons granulated sugar

⅓ cup Grand Marnier
Whipped cream

1. Wash and hull the strawberries. Drain.

2. Grate the orange peels, taking care not to include any of the white pith.

3. In a sturdy bowl, pound the sugar with the grated peel.

4. Squeeze the juice from the oranges and pour it over the peel and sugar. Stir well and add the Grand Marnier.

5. Pour the syrup over the strawberries and mix well. Allow to macerate for at least 1 hour. (The flavor will be more pronounced if the fruit is not refrigerated.) Serve with whipped cream.

⇓ ⇓ ⇓

⇟ ⇟ ⇟

THE MENU

Fish Terrine
Jambon Persillé
Tossed Green Salad with Vinaigrette Dressing
Baked Potato
Toasted Almond Parfait

This menu usually suggests Easter, but there is no reason why it should not be served at any other time of the year. Jambon Persillé is a traditional Easter dish of Burgundy. It is equally acceptable in May or September. Avoid making it when the humidity is high: Aspics and jellies do not weather well under these conditions. Jambon Persillé is perfectly beautiful in appearance and delightful to eat. Buy the best cooked ham possible. To accompany Jambon Persillé I usually offer a perfect baked potato without butter or sour cream.

Fish Terrine as an opener—small servings, please—starts the gastric juices flowing, and a simple parfait satisfies the need for something sweet, soothing, and cold.

THE INGREDIENTS

What You Will Need:

Baking potatoes
2 heads romaine lettuce
Salad greens
1 large bunch parsley
1 lemon
¾ pound fresh salmon, sliced thin
½ pound grey sole, filleted
4- to 5-pound Virginia or Smithfield ham
1 veal knuckle, chopped

2 calves' feet, boned
5 large eggs
1½ pints heavy cream
¼ pound unsalted butter
1 6-ounce package unskinned almonds
¾ cup maple syrup
2 pints vanilla ice cream
Dry white wine
Parchment paper

Staples to Have on Hand:

salt, white pepper, peppercorns, ground nutmeg, dried thyme, bay leaf, fresh tarragon, fresh chervil, Dijon mustard, white wine vinegar, red wine vinegar, olive oil

THE WORK SCHEDULE

3 Days Before Serving

1. Check the staples on hand and make your shopping list.
2. Order the fish, ham, veal knuckle, and calves' feet.
3. Buy the lettuce, salad greens, and herbs. Wash and dry. Store in sealed plastic bags in the refrigerator.

2 Days Before Serving

1. Buy the vanilla ice cream.
2. Toast the almonds, complete the parfaits, and freeze.
3. Begin the Jambon preparation through step 2 of the recipe. Cool, cover, and refrigerate.
4. Make the Vinaigrette Dressing (see page 282), pour it into a screw-top jar, and refrigerate.

1 Day Before Serving

1. Complete the Jambon Persillé (steps 3 through 5 of the recipe), cover, and refrigerate.
2. Prepare the Fish Terrine, cover, and refrigerate.
3. Set the table and select the wine.

Serving Day

1. *Two hours before serving,* unmold the Fish Terrine onto a serving platter. Return to the refrigerator until serving time.
2. *Two hours before serving,* unmold the Jambon Persillé onto a serving platter. Return to the refrigerator until serving time.
3. *One hour before serving,* preheat the oven to 425°F. and bake the potatoes.
4. *One half-hour before serving,* whip the cream and top the parfaits. Return to the refrigerator until serving time.
5. Arrange the salad ready for tossing.
6. Prepare the coffee maker and uncork the wine.

FISH TERRINE

4 tablespoons unsalted butter, softened
2 heads romaine lettuce
¾ pound fresh salmon, sliced thin
Salt
Freshly ground white pepper
½ pound grey sole, filleted

2 eggs
3 egg whites
1½ cups heavy cream
Ground nutmeg
Grated peel of 1 large lemon
¼ cup dry white wine

1. Preheat the oven to 300°F.

2. Butter a 6-cup terrine, preferably rectangular, with 2 tablespoons butter.

3. Remove the best and greenest of the romaine leaves and blanch them in boiling salted water. (Use 1 tablespoon salt for every quart of water.) Count to 30 and lift the leaves out with a skimmer. Drain.

4. Line the bottom and sides of the terrine with the blanched lettuce leaves. Arrange half the salmon slices on top of the leaves and sprinkle lightly with salt and pepper.

5. Put the sole in a food processor and blend until smooth and creamy. Add the eggs and egg whites and blend for 5 seconds. Add the cream slowly while blending. Add salt, pepper, and nutmeg to taste, and scrape the purée into a clean bowl. Add the grated lemon peel and mix thoroughly.

6. In a small saucepan bring 2 cups of water to a boil. Add 1 teaspoon salt. Poach 2 teaspoons of the fish purée in the water for 2 or 3 minutes. Test for seasoning. (This is the only control over the seasoning. Once the Terrine is put together, there is no way to correct it.)

7. Spoon the mixture into the prepared terrine and cover with the remaining salmon slices. Cover with more blanched lettuce leaves. Pour on the wine.

8. Melt the remaining butter and dribble it over the top. Cover with parchment paper and then with foil.

9. Put the terrine in a roasting pan and add enough hot water to come halfway up the sides of the terrine. Bake for 1 hour. Cool and turn out on a suitable platter. Serve either hot or cold.

JAMBON PERSILLÉ

1 4- to 5-pound Virginia or Smith-field ham
1 veal knuckle, chopped into pieces
2 calves' feet, boned and tied to-gether
2 quarts dry white wine
Bouquet garni consisting of: 2 or 3 small branches of tarragon, a few sprigs of chervil, 1 small bay leaf, a pinch of dried thyme, 3 to 4 parsley stalks, and 10 peppercorns tied in cheesecloth
2 tablespoons white wine vinegar
1 bunch parsley, coarsely chopped

1. In a ham kettle or large pan, cover the ham with cold water and bring slowly to a boil to get rid of the excess salt. You may have to repeat the operation if the ham is very salty.

2. When the "cleansing" is complete, cover the ham once again with cold water and bring slowly to a boil. Simmer very gently for 35 to 40 minutes. Cool, cover, and refrigerate.

3. Lift the ham out of the liquid and cut the meat off the bone in good-sized chunks. Put them in a clean pan with the knuckle of veal, calves' feet, and bouquet garni. Cover with the wine, bring to a boil, lower the heat, and simmer very gently for about an hour, skimming off the fat as it rises. The ham must be very thoroughly cooked, as it will be flaked later.

4. When you are satisfied that the ham is sufficiently cooked, pour off the liquid into a large mixing bowl through a strainer lined with three or four thicknesses of wet cheesecloth. Separate the ham from the veal and calves' feet. Stir 2 tablespoons of wine vinegar into the liquid and leave it to set slightly in the bowl or in a 4-quart mold.

5. Mash or flake the ham with a fork. It usually looks like coarse threads. Before the jelly sets, stir in the shredded ham and plenty of chopped parsley, ¾ cup at least. Pour over the ham in its bowl or mold. Stir to mix evenly. Refrigerate overnight to set.

6. To serve, turn out onto a large dish. Garnish with clumps of crisp, curly parsley. Serve with baked potatoes in their jackets.

TOASTED ALMOND PARFAIT

1 6-ounce package unskinned almonds   2 pints vanilla ice cream, softened
¾ cup or more maple syrup   Whipped cream

1. Preheat the oven to 400°F.

2. Spread the almonds on a baking sheet and toast them in the oven, turning them occasionally, until they are dark brown. Chop them very fine or put them through a food chopper.

3. Mix the almonds with the maple syrup to make a thin paste, adding more maple syrup if it seems too thick.

4. Spoon a generous tablespoon of the almond paste into the bottom of 6 to 8 parfait glasses or wine glasses. Cover with a thick layer of the ice cream. Continue in this manner until the glasses are full.

5. Cover the parfaits with plastic wrap and freeze. Remove them from the freezer 30 minutes before serving. Put them in the refrigerator. Top with the whipped cream.

⇃⇃⇃

THE MENU

Creamed Smoked Haddock
Virginia Ham and Cumberland Sauce
Ambrosia

An ideal supper menu, in my opinion, is one hot dish to start with, followed by a meat with a piquant sauce and fruit to wind up the meal—perfect for after the theater or concert. While the Creamed Smoked Haddock is being heated, there is time for a drink. The ham is already arranged on its serving dish, and the sauce is in its sauceboat. The Ambrosia is in the refrigerator. The entire meal can be on the table in 20 minutes at the most, the time it takes to reheat the fish dish.

THE INGREDIENTS

What You Will Need:

½ pound small mushrooms
1 lemon
4 oranges
2 grapefruit
2 bananas
2 pounds smoked haddock

Sliced ham from the delicatessen, or
  homemade
Unsalted butter
Milk
Red currant jelly
½ cup grated coconut

Staples to Have on Hand:

  salt, pepper, cayenne, ground nutmeg, Dijon mustard, red wine vinegar,
flour, port wine

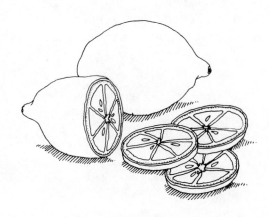

THE WORK SCHEDULE

2 Days Before Serving

1. Check the staples on hand and make your shopping list.
2. Buy everything you will need.
3. Prepare the Cumberland Sauce (see page 281), cool, and store in the refrigerator in a screw-top jar.

1 Day Before Serving

1. Prepare the fish for the Creamed Smoked Haddock (through step 3 of the recipe). Cover the fish and sauce and refrigerate them separately.
2. Prepare the citrus fruits for the Ambrosia (step 1 of the recipe) and refrigerate.
3. Set the table and select the wine.

Serving Day

1. *One half-hour before serving,* preheat the oven to 400°F. to cook the fish. Complete step 5 of the recipe and bake for 10 to 15 minutes, or until bubbling.
2. Pour the Cumberland Sauce into a sauceboat and take the ham out of the refrigerator.
3. Prepare the coffee maker and uncork the wine.
4. *Just before serving,* complete the Ambrosia by adding the sliced bananas and grated coconut.

CREAMED SMOKED HADDOCK

2 pounds smoked haddock to make
  approximately 4 cups cooked and
  flaked fish
Milk, sufficient to cover fish
3 tablespoons unsalted butter

3 tablespoons flour
Ground nutmeg
Freshly ground pepper
½ pound small mushrooms

1. Soak the haddock, in enough milk to cover it, for 1 hour; then bring the haddock and milk slowly to a boil in a heavy pan. Allow it to cool. When the haddock is cool enough to handle, drain and reserve the milk. You will need 2 cups of the milk later on. Remove the haddock's skin and all the bones.

2. Make a roux by melting the butter in a heavy pan and stirring in the flour. Cook gently for 2 to 3 minutes, being careful not to burn it. Remove from the heat.

3. Heat 2 cups of the milk in which the haddock was cooked and pour it into the roux all at once. Add the nutmeg and whisk until smooth. Return to gentle heat and cook for 5 to 6 minutes, stirring all the time. Correct the seasoning with the addition of freshly ground pepper. You will find that extra salt will not be necessary. Cool, cover, and refrigerate.

4. Preheat the oven to 400°F.

5. Wipe the mushrooms clean, cutting off the stems flush with the caps. If the mushrooms are large, halve or quarter them; the pieces should be no larger than a "quarter." Add them to the sauce and cook for 2 to 3 minutes longer. Stir the sauce into the flaked fish and pile it into an ovenproof dish. Bake for 10 to 15 minutes, or until bubbling.

VIRGINIA HAM AND CUMBERLAND SAUCE

2 slices ham per serving   Cumberland Sauce (see page 281)
Dijon mustard

1. Allow two thin slices of ham rather than a thick one for each serving, and a slice above the required number will do no harm. Ham of high quality can be bought at a good delicatessen if you have not already cooked one at home; avoid the supermarket wrapped product.

2. Arrange it on a serving platter, wrap in foil, and refrigerate it until serving time.

3. Serve with Dijon mustard and Cumberland Sauce.

⅄ ⅄ ⅄

AMBROSIA

2 grapefruit   2 bananas
3 oranges   ½ cup grated coconut

1. Peel grapefruit and oranges over a bowl to catch juices. Cut into segments, taking care that seeds do not fall into the bowl. This may be done early in the day.

2. Before serving, peel and slice the bananas and stir into the citrus fruits with the grated coconut.

⅄ ⅄ ⅄

⇟ ⇟ ⇟

THE MENU

Fish Mousse
Escalopes de Veau Normande
Trifle

There is a fish mousse to suit most purses, from the luxury of fresh salmon to almost any non-oily white fish. I have tested fish mousse with both; and, to tell the truth, I have difficulty deciding which is my favorite. Much depends on seasoning and the presentation.

The veal dish is a different matter. There is no substitute for fine milk-fed veal. It is an undeniable luxury. Escalopes de Veau is a table-side dish. Assemble everything that is needed and cook the escalopes in a chafing dish on a trolley or cart drawn up to the table.

Trifle is as English as John Bull, with as many variations and methods as there are colors in the rainbow. Most, in my opinion, are cloyingly rich, sodden with carelessly made custard, flavored with fruit juices and undrinkable sherry or white wine. The word trifle suggests something light—a mere trifle and nothing more. The recipe I give you has been in my family for more than a hundred years. It is simplicity personified and yet has great character: homemade sponge cakes, enough to fill a glass bowl; homemade raspberry jam; and a fine dry sherry worthy of Jerez. The entire confection is topped with sweetened whipped cream and sprinkled with toasted slivered almonds.

This menu has a touch of glamour; it is for very special occasions.

THE INGREDIENTS

What You Will Need:

3 shallots

1 lemon

6 apples

1 bunch parsley

2 pounds boneless non-oily fish

12 escalopes of veal

½ pound unsalted butter

1½ pints heavy cream

2 cups clam juice

Sponge cake or Genoise

Raspberry jam

½ cup slivered almonds

2 envelopes unflavored gelatin

Staples to Have on Hand:

salt, pepper, ground nutmeg, granulated sugar, confectioner's sugar, tomato paste, dry Madeira, Calvados or applejack, dry sherry, dry vermouth, dry white wine or cider, flour

THE WORK SCHEDULE

3 Days Before Serving
1. Check the staples on hand and make your shopping list.

2 Days Before Serving
1. Buy the staples you need: 1 pint of heavy cream, the apples, and the fish.
2. Poach the fish in seasoned water, cool, and flake. Cover and refrigerate.
3. Buy the sponge cake or make a Genoise.

1 Day Before Serving
1. Prepare the Fish Mousse, cover, and refrigerate.
2. Buy the veal.
3. Set the table and select the wine.

Serving Day
1. *Two hours before serving,* arrange the sponge cake sandwiches in a serving bowl (step 1 of the recipe). Do not refrigerate.
2. *Two hours before serving,* unmold the mousse, garnish, and put back in the refrigerator until serving time.
3. *One hour before serving,* drench the sponge cake sandwiches with the sherry. Whip the cream and mound it over the sandwiches. Sprinkle with the toasted almonds. Do not refrigerate again.
4. *One-half hour before serving,* peel and sauté the apples. Assemble all that is needed to prepare the Escalopes de Veau at the table just before serving.
5. Prepare the coffee maker and uncork the wine.

FISH MOUSSE

3 tablespoons finely chopped shallots
1 tablespoon unsalted butter
2 cups clam juice
2 envelopes unflavored gelatin, softened in ¼ cup dry vermouth
2 pounds boneless non-oily white fish, cooked and flaked enough to produce 2⅓ cups

1 tablespoon tomato paste
Salt, pepper, and ground nutmeg
3 tablespoons dry Madeira
2 tablespoons lemon juice
Grated peel of 1 lemon
¾ cup heavy cream
Parsley sprigs for garnish

1. Cook the shallots slowly in the butter till soft, taking care that they do not brown; otherwise the flavor will be altered. Add the clam juice and gelatin mixture and blend until smooth. Add the flaked fish, half at a time. (I find the blender produces a very fine purée.)

2. Empty into a clean bowl to cool. Add the tomato paste and season with salt, pepper, and nutmeg to taste. Season more than you would think necessary; the cream will tone it down.

3. Add the Madeira, lemon juice, and grated peel. When almost set, whip the cream until soft peaks form. Fold into the setting fish mixture. Correct the seasonings and spoon into an oiled 6-cup mold. (Use a decorative fish mold if you have one.) Cover and refrigerate. Garnish with parsley.

⇟ ⇟ ⇟

ESCALOPES DE VEAU NORMANDE

12 escalopes of veal
Flour for dredging
10 tablespoons unsalted butter
Salt and pepper
½ cup Calvados or applejack

½ cup dry white wine or cider
6 apples, peeled, cored, and quartered
2 to 3 tablespoons granulated sugar
½ cup heavy cream

1. Dredge escalopes with flour.

2. Heat 6 tablespoons of butter in a heavy skillet. Sauté the escalopes for 2 to 3 minutes, or until lightly browned. Season lightly with salt and pepper. Heat the Calvados, pour it over the veal and set it alight. When the flame dies down, add the wine and cook 2 minutes longer. Remove the veal to a heated platter and keep it warm while making the sauce and sautéing the apples.

3. In another skillet melt the remaining 4 tablespoons butter and sauté the apple quarters. Dust with a little sugar to glaze.

4. Add the cream to the other skillet. Blend well over gentle heat and season to taste. Pour the sauce over the escalopes and garnish with the apple quarters.

⅄ ⅄ ⅄

TRIFLE

1 sponge cake layer, homemade or bought from a reputable baker
Raspberry jam
Good dry sherry

1 cup heavy cream, whipped
2 tablespoons confectioner's sugar
½ cup slivered almonds, toasted

1. Cut the sponge cake into 4 × 2½-inch wedges. Split them lengthwise and spread with raspberry jam. Put the wedges together again to form sandwiches. Arrange the sandwiches in a serving bowl.

2. Pour enough sherry over the sandwiches to saturate them completely.

3. Beat the cream, and when soft peaks form, add the confectioner's sugar and beat again. Spoon over the soaked sponge cake, piling it high. Sprinkle with the toasted slivered almonds.

⇟⇟⇟

THE MENU

Mushroom Consommé
Collared Veal
Parsnip Purée
Rice Pudding de Luxe

Mushroom Consommé whets the appetite for what is to follow. I find it to be one of the most stimulating of consommés.

Collared Veal is an old English method for dealing with this much neglected cut. The anchovy has for centuries been much in evidence in English cookery. I believe it to be a throwback to the days when the island was occupied by the Romans who were addicted to a sauce called Garum, the principal ingredient being small fish in a state of fermentation. I am told it bore a strong resemblance to anchovy sauce. In any case, its presence in the filling for the shoulder of veal elevates the dish from the everyday to the sublime.

Once again I will drop a pearl of wisdom: When serving the dessert, make the portions small. It is rich and should be treated accordingly. The leftovers will find a place in the following day's menu.

THE INGREDIENTS

What You Will Need:

½ pound fresh mushrooms
3 pounds parsnips
1 bunch parsley
1 orange
6 slices white bread
1 half-shoulder of veal
2 ounces boiled ham
2 large eggs
3 cups milk

1 cup heavy cream
4 tablespoons unsalted butter
½ cup glacé fruits
½ ounce imported dry mushrooms
Flat anchovies
1½ teaspoons unflavored gelatin
Strawberries and whipped cream for
    garnish (optional)

Staples to Have on Hand:

   salt, pepper, ground mace, fresh chives, vanilla bean or vanilla extract,
long-grain rice; beef stock, veal or chicken stock; granulated sugar, Madeira,
kirsch

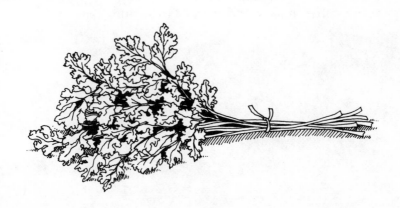

THE WORK SCHEDULE

2 Days Before Serving

1. Check the staples on hand and make your shopping list.
2. Buy everything you will need.
3. Soak the dried mushrooms for the Mushroom Consommé (step 1 of the recipe). Cover and refrigerate.

1 Day Before Serving

1. Prepare the filling for the veal, cover, and refrigerate (step 1 of the recipe).
2. Cook the parsnips (steps 1 and 2 of the recipe), cool, cover, and refrigerate.
3. Prepare the Rice Pudding, cover, and refrigerate.
4. Set the table and select the wine.

Serving Day

1. *Two hours before serving*, fill and tie the veal shoulder and begin the braising (steps 2 through 4 of the recipe).
2. Unmold the Rice Pudding, garnish if desired, and refrigerate until needed.
3. *One half-hour before serving*, transfer the parsnips to the top half of a double boiler. Reheat and season (step 3 of the recipe).
4. *Fifteen minutes before serving*, transfer the Mushroom Consommé to a pan, slice and add the fresh mushrooms, and complete step 2 of the recipe.
5. Prepare the coffee maker and uncork the wine.

MUSHROOM CONSOMMÉ

4 cups beef stock (see page 275)   Salt and pepper
½ ounce imported dry mushrooms   ¼ cup Madeira
½ pound fresh mushrooms   Finely chopped parsley

1. Bring 1 cup of the stock to a boil and pour over the dried mushrooms in a small bowl. Soak for 2 to 3 hours. Strain into the remaining stock, pressing out all the liquid. Discard the dried mushrooms.

2. Slice the fresh mushrooms very thin and add to what is now the consommé. Reheat, season with salt and pepper to taste, and add the Madeira. Before serving, garnish with finely chopped parsley.

⇟ ⇟ ⇟

COLLARED VEAL

STUFFING:
6 slices white bread, 1 to 2 days old if possible, crumbled
½ can flat anchovies, drained, rinsed, and chopped
1½ tablespoons chopped chives
4 tablespoons finely chopped parsley
1 teaspoon salt
¼ teaspoon freshly ground black pepper
4 tablespoons boiled ham, chopped fine
¼ teaspoon ground mace

VEAL:
1 half-shoulder of veal, boned (It should weigh not more than 6 pounds. The butcher will do the boning and trimming for you.)
3 tablespoons clarified butter (see page 282)
1 cup veal or chicken stock (see page 276)

(Continued)

1. In a bowl combine all the stuffing ingredients and mix well. Cover and refrigerate.

2. Lay the boned and trimmed shoulder out flat. Spread the filling evenly over the inside of the shoulder to within 2 inches of the edges. Roll up loosely and neatly and tie in the shape of a sausage. Dust the outside lightly with salt and pepper.

3. Preheat the oven to 375°F.

4. Melt the butter in a heavy skillet and brown the rolled veal well on all sides. If this has been done in a casserole with a lid, add the stock, cover, and put in the oven. If not, transfer it to one. Cook for 1½ hours. Roll it over in its casserole occasionally. Remove the veal to a warm platter and reduce the juices in the pan to make a sauce. To serve, cut the string and carve.

⚡ ⚡ ⚡

PARSNIP PURÉE

3 pounds parsnips	Salt and pepper
4 tablespoons unsalted butter	¼ cup cream
Grated peel of 1 orange	Finely chopped parsley

1. Peel parsnips and cut into quarters, removing the woodlike core. Dice and cook slowly in a little salted water.

2. Purée in a food processor or food mill with the butter. Stir in grated orange peel and season with salt and pepper to taste. This can be done ahead. Cool, cover, and refrigerate.

3. To serve, reheat, stir in cream and finely chopped parsley.

⚡ ⚡ ⚡

RICE PUDDING DE LUXE

½ cup finely chopped glacé fruits
3 tablespoons kirsch
½ cup long-grain rice
3 cups milk
¼ teaspoon salt
1½ teaspoons unflavored gelatin
2 tablespoons water

2 egg yolks
¼ cup granulated sugar
1 3-inch piece vanilla bean, or
   1½ teaspoons vanilla extract
½ cup heavy cream, whipped
Strawberries and whipped cream for
   garnish (optional)

1. Marinate the glacé fruits in the kirsch. Soak the rice in hot water for ½ hour. Drain.

2. In a heavy saucepan combine 2 cups of milk, the salt and the rice and bring to a boil. Reduce the heat and simmer gently, covered, for approximately 20 minutes. Add a little more milk if it seems to be drying out.

3. Sprinkle the gelatin over the water in a small bowl. Let stand for 3 to 4 minutes, or until soft.

4. Separate the eggs and beat the yolks lightly with the sugar. Stir in the remaining cup of milk. Pour into the top half of double boiler standing in hot water. Over gentle heat, cook, while stirring, until thickened. The mixture should generously coat the back of a wooden spoon. Add the softened gelatin. Stir until dissolved and strain into the rice mixture. Mix and chill until it begins to set. Fold in the marinated fruits and vanilla extract.

5. Whip the cream until soft peaks form. Fold into the rice mixture and spoon into a lightly oiled 1-quart mold or soufflé dish. Chill for at least 4 hours.

6. Unmold and garnish to your liking. I suggest fresh strawberries and rosettes of whipped cream.

↯ ↯ ↯

THE MENU

Carrots Rapées
Vitello Tonnato
Frozen Coffee Mousse

This is one of my favorite summer menus. It proceeds from what could be a vegetarian restaurant's dish to a coffee mousse that is capable of weaning a waist watcher from his best intentions. It is a menu for the dog days of August and one that never fails to please.

THE INGREDIENTS

What You Will Need:

4 stalks celery
1 large onion
Carrots (for quantity, see page 185)
3 lemons
1 bunch parsley
3- to 4-pound boneless roast of veal
  cut from leg

½ dozen large eggs
½ pint heavy cream
1 7-ounce can tuna fish in oil
1 small can anchovy fillets
Cooked white rice
Dry white wine
Semisweet chocolate (optional)

Staples to Have on Hand:

  salt, pepper, white pepper, peppercorns, garlic cloves, red wine vinegar,
vegetable oil, olive oil, capers, sour pickles, instant coffee powder, granulated
sugar, confectioner's sugar, vanilla extract

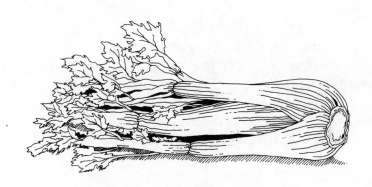

THE WORK SCHEDULE

3 Days Before Serving
1. Check the staples on hand and make your shopping list.
2. Buy everything you will need.

2 Days Before Serving
1. Prepare Vitello Tonnato through step 2 of the recipe. Cook and allow the veal to cool in its liquid. Cover and refrigerate.
2. Prepare the Coffee Mousse and freeze it in individual ramekins.

1 Day Before Serving
1. Take the veal out of its liquid and set aside. Put the pan with its liquid back on the stove and reduce until you have 2 cups. Strain and refrigerate until following day (step 3 of the recipe).
2. Slice veal and wrap securely before refrigerating.
3. Grate the carrots. Wrap and refrigerate.
4. Prepare the dressing for the Carrots Rapées (step 2 of the recipe).
5. Boil eggs for Vitello Tonnato garnish.
6. Cook rice, strain, cool, and refrigerate.
7. Set the table and select the wine.

Serving Day
1. Finish the sauce for the Vitello Tonnato. By now it should be jellied.
2. *One hour before serving,* assemble the veal dish, complete the garnish, and refrigerate until needed.
3. Garnish the Coffee Mousse.
4. Prepare the coffee maker and uncork the wine.
5. *Just before serving,* toss the carrots with the dressing and garnish.

✲✲✲

CARROTS RAPÉES

Carrots
¼ cup red wine vinegar
¼ teaspoon salt
½ teaspoon granulated sugar (optional)
¼ teaspoon white pepper
½ cup vegetable oil
½ cup olive oil
2 tablespoons finely chopped parsley

1. Grate the carrots on the coarsest side of a grater or put them through the coarsest disc of a food processor. Cover and refrigerate until needed.

2. Combine the vinegar, salt, sugar, pepper, and oils in a screw-top jar. Shake just before pouring over the carrots. Toss the dressing and the carrots together and sprinkle with parsley just before serving.

Note: The number of carrots needed will depend on their size; choose small when possible. The dressing will coat 6 to 8 servings.

VITELLO TONNATO

1 3- to 4-pound boneless piece of solid veal, cut from the leg, tied with string
1 7-ounce can tuna fish in oil
1 small can anchovy fillets
2 cups dry white wine
½ sour pickle, coarsely chopped
2 carrots
1 large onion
4 stalks celery
2 cloves garlic
8 peppercorns
4 to 5 sprigs parsley
Mayonnaise (see page 280)
Lemon juice
Cooked rice
2 tablespoons capers
Yolks of 2 hard-boiled eggs
Finely chopped parsley

1. Place the veal in a large, heavy saucepan with water barely to cover.

2. Drain and flake the tuna. Drain the anchovy fillets and chop coarsely. Add both to the saucepan. Add the wine and the pickle. Coarsely chop the carrots, onion, celery and garlic and tie in a piece of cheesecloth with the peppercorns and the parsley. Add to the pan, and bring the liquid to a boil. Lower heat to

(Continued)

simmer and cook for 1½ hours. Remove from the heat and cool the veal in the stock. Remove the veal, cut off the strings, and set aside. Remove the cheesecloth bag and discard.

3. Place the saucepan of stock over high heat and reduce the liquid by boiling rapidly to about 2 cups of strong stock. Strain the stock through several layers of cheesecloth into a mixing bowl and allow to cool. Chill until set as a jelly.

4. Stir sufficient mayonnaise into the jellied stock to make a heavy masking sauce. Season to taste with lemon juice.

5. Cut the veal into ¼-inch-thick slices. Make a mound of your favorite cooked rice on a large serving platter and cover the rice with the sliced veal. Pour the sauce over the veal slices. Scatter the capers on top.

6. Press the egg yolks through a fine sieve. Sprinkle a border of finely chopped parsley around the edge of the dish, and inside of that a border of sieved egg yolk.

⇓ ⇓ ⇓

FROZEN COFFEE MOUSSE

4 eggs, separated
6 tablespoons granulated sugar
3 tablespoons instant coffee powder
Salt
1 cup heavy cream

¼ teaspoon vanilla extract
2 tablespoons confectioner's sugar
Grated semisweet chocolate for garnish (optional)

1. Put the egg yolks into a stainless steel bowl. Beat the yolks with 4 tablespoons sugar until pale yellow. Set over barely simmering water and continue to beat until thick. Add the instant coffee and beat until blended.

2. Whip the egg whites with a pinch of salt until frothy. Add the remaining 2 tablespoons sugar and beat until a soft meringue forms. Mix one-third of this into the yolk mixture, then fold in the rest. Set the mixture over ice and beat until cool.

3. Whip the cream and vanilla until almost firm. Sprinkle in confectioner's sugar and beat. Fold into the mousse. Freeze until firm. Decorate with grated semisweet chocolate.

⅄⅄⅄

THE MENU

Champignons sous Cloche
Curried Vegetables with Rice
Pineapple with Kirsch

Since the formation of the East India Company in the eighteenth century, curry has been almost as closely associated with the British Isles as with India. But there is a difference: Few British cooks took the time or the trouble to blend freshly ground spices. Instead, they relied almost solely on imported canned mixtures which when fresh had fragrance, but when exposed to air lost their aroma to evaporation. They were a poor substitute, indeed.

For the following Curry Sauce I use either an imported canned blend or, when I can find it, a curry paste submerged in oil. The sauce freezes well and provides a base for cold meats—beef, lamb or chicken—or freshly prepared vegetables. The result is a satisfying, economical entrée when served with plain boiled rice.

Mushrooms sous Cloche is an adaptation of the original recipe in which the mushrooms were baked under a glass bell—but who in this day and age has an adequate supply of glass bells? A shallow pyrex dish serves the purpose when covered with metal foil and sealed.

A dessert of peeled, cored, and sliced pineapple sprinkled with kirsch is perfect after almost any curried dish. The pineapple slices are improved when the kirsch is allowed to act as a marinade.

THE INGREDIENTS

What You Will Need:

1 pound mushrooms
6 medium carrots
4 celery stalks
1 small head cauliflower
4 small zucchini
1 small onion
1 lemon
1 lime
1 bunch parsley sprigs

2 ripe pineapples
¼ pound unsalted butter
½ cup heavy cream
3½ cups cooked rice
2 dried apricots
⅓ cup raisins
1 long loaf French or Italian bread
Lager or light beer

Staples to Have on Hand:

salt, white pepper, dried chervil, curry powder, garlic clove, vegetable oil, chicken stock (see page 276), flour, superfine sugar, dry sherry, kirsch

THE WORK SCHEDULE

3 Days Before Serving
1. Check the staples on hand and make your shopping list.
2. Buy the pineapples to allow them time to ripen to perfection.

2 Days Before Serving
1. Buy the vegetables with the exception of the mushrooms. Wash, dry, and store in sealed plastic bags in the refrigerator.
2. Prepare the curry sauce (step 3 of the recipe). Cool, cover, and refrigerate.

1 Day Before Serving
1. Prepare and blanch the vegetables. Dry thoroughly and store in sealed plastic bags in the refrigerator.
2. Buy carefully selected mushrooms and French bread.
3. Assemble the mushroom dish (through step 4 of the recipe). Cover and refrigerate.
4. Peel and slice the pineapples. Cut out their center cores with a small cookie cutter. Wrap the pineapple slices securely and refrigerate.
5. Buy beer or lager to serve with the curry. Set the table.

Serving Day
1. *One hour before serving,* sprinkle the pineapple with kirsch and return to the refrigerator.
2. *One half-hour before serving,* preheat the oven to 375°F. for the mushroom dish and complete steps 6 and 7 of the recipe.
3. *One half-hour before serving,* cook the rice and keep it hot in the oven or in a colander over a pan of hot water.
4. *Fifteen minutes before serving,* reheat the curry sauce and complete steps 4 through 6 of the recipe.
5. Prepare the coffee maker.

☙ ☙ ☙

CHAMPIGNONS SOUS CLOCHE

8 slices crusty bread, cut from the wide part of a loaf of French or Italian bread
6 tablespoons unsalted butter
1½ tablespoons lemon juice
½ teaspoon dried chervil
½ teaspoon salt
⅛ teaspoon white pepper
1 pound mushrooms
8 tablespoons heavy cream
8 teaspoons dry sherry
Parsley sprigs for garnish

1. Toast the bread.

2. In a bowl, whip the butter for a few minutes until it is fluffy. Beat in the lemon juice, chervil, salt, and pepper. Spread the bread generously with this mixture.

3. Put the slices in eight individual baking dishes or in an oblong shallow earthenware or pyrex dish.

4. Cut the stems from the mushrooms flush with the caps. Butter the tops of the caps with the seasoned butter. Arrange the caps, round side up, to form a mound on each piece of toast. Cool, cover, and refrigerate.

5. Preheat the oven to 375°F.

6. Spoon a little heavy cream over each mound of mushrooms. Cover the dish or dishes with foil and bake for 25 minutes.

7. Before serving, remove the foil and pour a teaspoonful of sherry over each mound of mushrooms. Garnish with parsley and serve at once.

CURRIED VEGETABLES

6 medium carrots
4 celery stalks
4 small zucchini
1 small head cauliflower
2 tablespoons vegetable oil
2 tablespoons chopped onion
3 tablespoons curry powder
2 tablespoons flour

1 small garlic clove, peeled and
   crushed
2 dried apricots, chopped fine
3½ cups chicken stock (see page 276)
⅓ cup raisins
1 tablespoon lime juice
3½ cups cooked rice
1 cup parsley sprigs, chopped

1. Wash the vegetables thoroughly under cold running water. Scrape the carrots and cut them on the bias into 1-inch pieces. Scrape the celery with a vegetable peeler to remove any coarse fibers and cut it into pieces to match the carrots. Cut the ends off the zucchini and quarter them lengthwise. Divide the cauliflower into bite-sized pieces.

2. Bring to a boil 1 quart of water to which 1 tablespoon of salt has been added. Cook the carrots for 4 to 5 minutes, lift out and drain. Cook the celery for 3 to 4 minutes, lift out and drain. Cook the cauliflower for 4 to 5 minutes, lift out and drain. Test each vegetable while cooking to be sure it remains crisp. Cool, cover, and refrigerate.

3. Heat the oil in a heavy saucepan. Add the onion and cook, stirring, for several minutes; do not let the onion burn. Stir in the curry powder and flour and cook for 2 minutes. Add the garlic and apricots. Remove from the heat and pour in the stock. Return to a gentle heat and whisk until thick. Stir in the raisins. Cool, cover, and refrigerate.

4. Reheat the curry sauce and add the zucchini. Simmer for 3 to 4 minutes.

5. Add the prepared vegetables and simmer for 6 to 7 minutes to allow the vegetables to absorb the flavor of the curry.

6. Stir in the lime juice just before serving. Pile the curried vegetables in the middle of a serving dish with rice at either end. Sprinkle generously with chopped parsley.

PINEAPPLE WITH KIRSCH

2 ripe pineapples   Superfine sugar
½ cup kirsch

1. Peel and core both pineapples and cut each into 8 slices. Pour the kirsch over the slices and refrigerate for at least 1 hour.

2. Serve cold, dusted with a little fine sugar.

⇟ ⇟ ⇟

THE MENU

Jellied Watercress Soup
Gnocchi Parisienne with Chicken Liver Sauce
Green Salad with Vinaigrette Dressing
Poires Noires

It took time to convince me that Gnocchi Parisienne would tolerate freezing and stand up to reheating; but when it was put to the test, it was impossible to tell that the gnocchi had not been freshly made to order. To freeze, brush each separate "dumpling"—for that is what it is—with melted butter; freeze till hard, wrap and seal securely. To serve, defrost the gnocchi, arrange them in a serving dish, cover them with the sauce, and bake them.

I created Poires Noires some years ago for teenagers with hearty appetites and a sweet tooth. But after the recipe appeared in a national publication, I was so swamped with mail that I decied to include it in my school's repertoire.

Jellied Watercress Soup is a splendid standby. The chicken stock must be strong; otherwise it won't jell. A small veal bone added to the other stock ingredients will assure this. For those who prefer the soup less peppery, cut down on the amount of watercress—say 1 cup for every quart of chicken stock.

THE INGREDIENTS

What You Will Need:

1 bunch watercress
3 mushrooms
Parsley sprigs
Salad greens
2 lemons
6 firm Anjou or Comice pears, with
    stems intact
6 chicken livers

½ pound unsalted butter
4 large eggs
2 ounces Parmesan cheese
4 ounces unsweetened chocolate
2 ounces semisweet chocolate
Bovril
Crystallized mint (optional)

Staples to Have on Hand:

salt, pepper, cayenne, cinnamon sticks, whole cloves, Dijon mustard, garlic clove, red wine vinegar, olive oil, tomato paste, chicken stock (see page 276), flour, granulated sugar, dry red wine

THE WORK SCHEDULE

3 Days Before Serving

1. Check the staples on hand and make your shopping list.
2. Buy everything you will need with the exception of the pears, the salad greens, and the parsley.

2 Days Before Serving

1. Buy the pears, the salad greens, and the parsley. Choose pears that are not overripe.
2. Prepare the Watercress Soup, cover, and refrigerate.
3. Poach the pears in the syrup (through step 3 of the recipe). Cool, cover, and refrigerate them in the syrup.

1 Day Before Serving

1. Prepare the gnocchi completely and the Chicken Liver Sauce (step 1 of the recipe). Spoon the sauce over the gnocchi; cool, cover, and refrigerate.
2. Prepare the Vinaigrette Dressing (see page 282) for the salad.
3. Chill the bowl for the soup.
4. Set the table and select the wine.

Serving Day

1. Remove the pears from the refrigerator and drain them until they are dry. Melt the chocolate and coat the pears. Refrigerate the pears until serving time.
2. *Two hours before baking,* remove the gnocchi from the refrigerator.
3. *Thirty minutes before serving,* preheat the oven 350°F. and warm the gnocchi for 20 minutes.
4. Arrange the pears in a serving dish.
5. Arrange the salad ready for tossing.
6. Prepare the coffee maker and uncork the wine.
7. *Just before serving,* garnish the soup.

JELLIED WATERCRESS SOUP

2 cups watercress leaves, about ¾ of a bunch
4 cups chicken stock (see page 276)
Salt, pepper, and lemon juice to taste

Yolk of 1 hard-boiled egg, sieved, for garnish
Finely chopped parsley for garnish

1. Purée the watercress leaves with 1 cup of stock. Stir into the remaining stock and season with salt, pepper, and lemon juice to taste.

2. Return to refrigerator to reset.

3. To serve, spoon into cold cups. Garnish with sieved egg yolk and finely chopped parsley.

⇊ ⇊ ⇊

GNOCCHI PARISIENNE

3 tablespoons unsalted butter
1 cup water
4 tablespoons grated Parmesan cheese
Salt and cayenne

½ teaspoon Dijon mustard
1 cup flour
3 eggs
Chicken Liver Sauce (see following recipe)

1. Melt the butter in the water with the cheese, salt and cayenne to taste, and the mustard. Bring to a boil and add the flour all at once. Remove from the heat and stir until the mixture leaves the sides of the pan.

2. Turn into a bowl and, when cooled, beat in the eggs one at a time, making sure each egg has been absorbed before the next is added.

3. With two hot, wet spoons, mold the paste into egg shapes and drop into simmering salted water. The gnocchi are done when they rise to the top. Drain on a linen towel or on paper towels.

4. To freeze, put drained dumplings on a cookie sheet and brush each with melted butter. Freeze until hard. Wrap securely and return to freezer.

CHICKEN LIVER SAUCE FOR GNOCCHI

6 chicken livers
1 small clove garlic
3 tablespoons unsalted butter
3 mushrooms, sliced
1 teaspoon tomato paste

1 teaspoon meat glaze (Bovril)
3 tablespoons flour
1½ cups chicken stock (see page 276)
2 tablespoons dry red wine
½ cup grated Parmesan cheese

1. Sauté the chicken livers and garlic in 2 tablespoons butter. Add the mushrooms, tomato paste, and meat glaze. Remove from the heat and blend in the flour. Add the stock and wine. Return to the heat and stir until thick. Check the seasoning—it should be very pronounced.

2. Arrange the gnocchi on the bottom of a shallow, well-buttered ovenproof dish. Sprinkle with a little grated cheese. Pour the sauce over the gnocchi and sprinkle with the remaining cheese. Dot with the remaining butter. Cool, cover, and refrigerate.

3. Preheat the oven to 350°F.

4. Bake for 20 minutes, or until hot and bubbling.

⚓ ⚓ ⚓

POIRES NOIRES

1 cup sugar
4 cups water
Juice of 1 lemon
2 sticks cinnamon
4 whole cloves
6 firm pears with stems intact (Anjou
   or Comice)

4 (4 ounces) squares unsweetened
   chocolate
2 (2 ounces) squares semisweet
   chocolate
¼ cup (½ stick) unsalted butter,
   softened
Crystallized mint (optional)

1. Dissolve the sugar in the water; add the lemon juice and spices and simmer in a pan with a tightly fitting lid for 10 to 15 minutes. *(Continued)*

2. Peel the pears carefully and cut a slice off the bottom of each so that they will remain upright. Leave stems intact.

3. Poach them gently in the boiling syrup until tender, 30 to 40 minutes. Time will depend on the ripeness of the pears. Test with a toothpick if you are in doubt. Allow the pears to cool thoroughly in the syrup, preferably overnight.

4. Melt all the chocolate in a bowl over warm water. Add the butter and stir until butter is melted and the mixture is smooth.

5. Remove the chilled pears from the syrup and dry gently. Dip the pears in the melted chocolate to coat evenly. (Use a spoon if necessary.) Lift pears to drain off excess chocolate and arrange them on a serving dish—preferably a white one.

6. Decorate the top of each pear with a sprig of crystallized mint or any suitable greenery you may happen to have. The pears will keep satisfactorily for up to 36 hours. After that, they are inclined to weep.

SPECIAL OCCASION
MENUS

↯ ↯ ↯

JULY FOURTH

Shrimp Scandia
Roast Chicken
Spaghetti Squash
Sabayon Frappé aux Pêches

I can see no point having a cook-out on July 4th. The variety of possibilities is not nearly wide enough. A clambake would be much appreciated, but that is a major undertaking.

My suggested menu is something different from the traditional barbecue, but just as simple to prepare. Peaches are at their best about now, and spaghetti squash is in the stores—make use of both while you can.

THE INGREDIENTS

What You Will Need:

1 small onion
1 celery stalk
2 lemons
1 orange (optional)
1 3-pound spaghetti squash
1 bunch watercress
Fresh dill

2 peaches
1 3-pound roasting chicken
1½ pounds small shrimp
½ pound Virginia or Smithfield ham
¼ pound unsalted butter
Large eggs
½ pint heavy cream

Staples to Have on Hand:

salt, coarse salt, pepper, white pepper, peppercorns, grated nutmeg, garlic clove, Dijon mustard, red wine vinegar, vegetable oil, granulated sugar, Madeira

THE WORK SCHEDULE

2 Days Before Serving

1. Check the staples on hand and make your shopping list.
2. Order the chicken and shrimp to be picked up the following day.
3. Buy everything else you will need.

1 Day Before Serving

1. Pick up the chicken and shrimp.
2. Make the Sauce Scandia (see page 282).
3. Prepare the sabayon and complete the dessert.
4. Cook the shrimp, cover, and refrigerate.
5. Set the table and select the wine.

Serving Day

1. *One and one-half hours before serving,* preheat the oven to 400°F. and prepare the chicken for the oven (steps 2 and 3 of the recipe). Roast for 1 hour (step 4).
2. The spaghetti squash may be baked in the same oven as the chicken and at the same time, but for only 45 minutes.
3. Complete the shrimp dish and arrange it on a serving platter.
4. Prepare the coffee maker and uncork the wine.
5. Serve the sabayon directly from the freezer.

SHRIMP SCANDIA

COURT BOUILLON (poaching liquid):
1 small onion, chopped
1 celery stalk, chopped
1 tablespoon salt
4 peppercorns
1 quart water

SHRIMP:
1½ pounds small shrimp (25 to 30 to the pound), shelled and deveined
Sauce Scandia (see page 282)

1. Combine all the ingredients for the court bouillon in a 2-quart pot. Bring to a boil, lower the heat, and simmer, covered, for 20 minutes or so. Strain the liquid into a clean pot, discard the solids, and bring to a boil once more.

2. Add the shrimp and bring to a boil again. Remove from the heat. Drain after 2 or 3 minutes. Cool.

3. Prepare the Sauce Scandia.

4. Toss the cold shrimp in enough sauce to coat well, and serve the shrimp on toothpicks.

ROAST CHICKEN

1 3-pound roasting chicken
Coarse salt
1 clove garlic

Juice of 1 lemon
Freshly ground pepper

1. Preheat the oven to 400°F.

2. Wipe the inside of the chicken with a damp cloth or paper towel. Sprinkle inside and out very generously with coarse salt. Peel the garlic clove, chop fine,

and, using a small knife as a palette knife, crush it to a paste with 2 teaspoons of coarse salt. Rub the inside of the chicken with half the garlic paste.

3. Truss or tie up the chicken for the oven and smear the rest of the paste on the outside of the bird. Place it on a rack in a roasting pan. Pour half the lemon juice inside the chicken and pat the remainder all over it. Dust with a little more coarse salt and freshly ground black pepper.

4. Cook for 1 hour in the middle of the oven, without basting. Do not open the door.

SPAGHETTI SQUASH

1 3-pound spaghetti squash	Salt and pepper
4 tablespoons unsalted butter	Grated nutmeg
½ pound Virginia or Smithfield ham, diced	A few sprigs of watercress for garnish

1. Preheat the oven to 400°F.

2. Bake the squash whole for approximately 45 minutes, or until it looks ready to collapse. Cut it in half and remove seeds. Scrape out the pulp (it will shred and look exactly like spaghetti) into a bowl. Stir in the butter and diced ham, and season with salt, pepper, and nutmeg to taste.

3. Reheat slowly and serve in a suitable dish garnished with a few watercress sprigs.

SABAYON FRAPPÉ AUX PÊCHES

3 egg yolks
1 egg
½ cup granulated sugar
4 to 8 tablespoons Madeira
½ cup heavy cream, beaten stiff

1 teaspoon grated orange or lemon
   peel
2 peaches
¼ cup granulated sugar
½ cup water

1. Beat the egg yolks, egg, ½ cup sugar, and Madeira in a large ceramic bowl until well blended. Put the bowl over a pan of simmering water and whisk until frothy and stiff. Remove from the pan, put in cold water, and beat the mixture until it is cold. Fold in the beaten cream and grated peel.

2. Put the peaches in boiling water for 5 minutes. Remove, peel, and slice them. If the peaches are unripe, put them in a pan with ¼ cup sugar and ½ cup water and simmer slowly for 10 to 15 minutes, or until they are tender. Drain and cool.

3. Put the peach slices on the bottom of a serving dish or individual dishes. Chill. Then pour the Sabayon over the peaches and freeze for at least 1 hour before serving.

⇊ ⇊ ⇊

THANKSGIVING

Pumpkin Soup
Casserole of Turkey and Chestnuts
Braised Celery
Purée of Carrots
Fresh Fruits
Mince Pies

Tradition is hard to break. I was anxious to avoid roast turkey yet wanted to use turkey for the menu, so I came up with this casserole with chestnuts. Pumpkin makes its appearance here as soup. For dessert—and to decorate the table—we have fresh fruits, a tradition and something sweet, and mince pies. Mincemeat improves with keeping; I am right now using some made eighteen years ago.

THE INGREDIENTS

What You Will Need:

Fruits
2 pounds fresh pumpkin
18 medium carrots
1 bunch parsley sprigs
½ pound chestnuts
3 celery hearts
1 lemon
5 pounds raw turkey breast (or the frozen "turkey roast" sold in supermarkets)

½ cup Virginia ham
Milk
1½ cups sour cream
⅓ cup heavy cream
½ pound unsalted butter
Eggs
Bovril
1 ounce dried mushrooms
2 14- to 15-ounce jars mincemeat
White Bordeaux wine

Staples to Have on Hand:

   salt, pepper, ground ginger, ground cinnamon, garlic cloves, tomato paste, chicken stock (see page 276), onion, flour, brown sugar, superfine sugar, dark rum, brandy

THE WORK SCHEDULE

3 Days Before Serving

1. Check the staples on hand and make your shopping list.
2. Buy everything you will need.

2 Days Before Serving

1. Make the pastry (see page 52) and bake the mincemeat pies. Store in airtight containers, but do not refrigerate.
2. Peel the chestnuts (see recipe for instructions).
3. Make the Pumpkin Soup (steps 1 and 2 of the recipe). Cool, cover, and refrigerate.

1 Day Before Serving

1. Prepare the turkey casserole, but do not add the sour cream. Cool, cover, and refrigerate.
2. Make the Purée of Carrots.
3. Prepare and boil the celery hearts (steps 1 and 2 of the recipe). Drain well, cool, cover, and refrigerate.
4. Set the table, select the wine, and arrange the fresh fruits.

Serving Day

1. *One hour before serving,* preheat the oven to 350°F. Reheat the turkey casserole for 35 to 40 minutes.
2. *Forty-five minutes before serving,* preheat the oven to 350°F. and complete steps 4 and 5 of the Braised Celery recipe.
3. Reheat the pumpkin soup (step 3 of the recipe).
4. Reheat the Carrot Purée in the top half of a double boiler.
5. Prepare the coffee maker and uncork the wine.
6. Mince pies may be heated slowly before serving for better flavor.

↯ ↯ ↯

PUMPKIN SOUP

2 pounds fresh pumpkin, with peel
  and seeds removed
2 cups water
3 cups milk
2 tablespoons brown sugar
1 tablespoon unsalted butter

Salt and pepper
Ground ginger
Ground cinnamon
½ cup Virginia ham, finely julienned
Finely chopped parsley

1. Cut the pumpkin into chunks and simmer in water until tender, for about 5 minutes. Drain. Purée the pumpkin in a blender or rub it through a fine sieve.

2. Heat the milk in a heavy pan. Stir in the pumpkin purée, brown sugar, and butter. Season to taste with salt and pepper. Add very little ginger and cinnamon. Heat, but do not allow to boil. Cool, cover, and refrigerate.

3. To serve, reheat over a very low flame so that the soup does not stick to the pan. Divide the julienne of ham between the soup bowls. Ladle in the soup and garnish with a little chopped parsley.

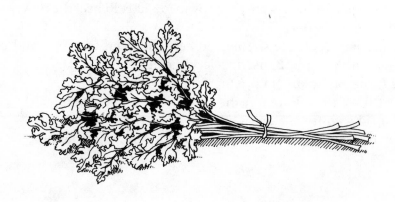

CASSEROLE OF TURKEY AND CHESTNUTS

1 ounce dried mushrooms
1 cup boiling water
8 tablespoons unsalted butter
5 pounds raw turkey breast, cut into
   1-inch cubes
6 tablespoons brandy
2 tablespoons finely chopped onion
4 cloves garlic, chopped
2 teaspoons meat glaze (Bovril)
2 tablespoons tomato paste
6 tablespoons flour

2 cups chicken (see page 276) or
   turkey stock
1 cup dry white Bordeaux wine
Salt and pepper
½ pound cooked chestnuts, cut into
   ¼-inch dice (Slit the chestnuts in
   the shape of a cross, roast them for
   30 minutes in a 375°F. oven, then
   peel and dice.)
1½ cups sour cream
½ cup finely chopped parsley

1. One hour before preparing, cover the dried mushrooms with 1 cup boiling water and set aside.

2. Preheat the oven to 350°F.

3. Cut the turkey or turkey roast into 1-inch cubes. Melt the butter in a skillet and brown the turkey cubes, a few at a time. Add a little more butter during the browning, if necessary. Transfer the cubes as they are done to an ovenproof casserole with a lid. After all the turkey has been browned and placed in the casserole, put the skillet over low heat and add the brandy to whatever juices there are in the skillet, scraping to loosen the bits which have stuck to the side during the process of browning.

4. Drain the mushrooms, reserving the liquid. Chop them finely and add them with the onion and garlic to the liquid in the skillet. Stir in the meat glaze, tomato paste, and flour, mixing thoroughly over low heat. Gradually add the mushroom liquid, chicken stock and wine. Cook the mixture slowly, stirring constantly, until the sauce thickens. Season with salt and pepper to taste, then pour the sauce over the turkey in the casserole and mix in the cooked chestnuts.

5. Cover and bake for 35 minutes, or until tender. Stir in the sour cream and reheat very briefly. After the sour cream has been added, don't allow it to come to a boil again, as it will curdle. Sprinkle with the chopped parsley just before serving. If the casserole is to be frozen or refrigerated, do not stir in the sour cream until it has been defrosted and/or reheated.

BRAISED CELERY

½ celery heart per serving or 4 celery
   stalks
Softened unsalted butter
Salt and pepper

¼ cup chicken stock (see page 276)
Juice of 1 lemon
Finely chopped parsley

1. Preheat the oven to 350°F.

2. Prepare the celery hearts by scraping the outside with a vegetable peeler. If celery stalks are used, treat in the same way, but cut them into 2-inch pieces on the bias.

3. Boil the celery in plenty of boiling salted water for 20 minutes. Lift out the celery and drain.

4. Butter an ovenproof dish with a cover. Arrange the hearts or stalks in the dish; dot with butter, and season lightly with salt and pepper. Pour in the chicken stock.

5. Cover and bake for 30 minutes. Before serving, sprinkle with the juice of 1 lemon and finely chopped parsley.

Note: Canned celery hearts can be substituted for the fresh.

⇟ ⇟ ⇟

PURÉE OF CARROTS

3 medium carrots per person
3 to 4 tablespoons unsalted butter
Granulated sugar (optional)

Grated peel of 1 lemon or orange
Salt and pepper

1. Wash and peel the carrots. If large, quarter each one and cut out the woody center. Chop coarsely.

2. In a heavy pan add half the butter, 2 tablespoons water, and a little sugar.

3. Cover and cook until tender over very low heat.

4. Purée with the remaining butter. Stir in grated peel and reheat. Season with salt and pepper to taste.

⇊⇊⇊

MINCE PIES

2 recipes short pastry (see page 52)
2 14- to 15-ounce jars of mincemeat
½ cup dark rum

2 egg yolks beaten well with ⅓ cup
   heavy cream
Superfine sugar

1. Preheat the oven to 375°F.

2. Butter, then line a 15¾ × 10½-inch baking sheet with an edge with half the short pastry rolled out to a thickness of approximately ⅛ inch, allowing about half an inch to hang over the edge all the way around. Bake for 10 minutes.

3. Mix the 2 jars of mincemeat with the rum and spread the mixture evenly over the pastry-lined baking sheet. Roll out the remaining pastry and cover the mincemeat, pinching the unbaked and half-baked pastry edges together carefully. Brush the top with the egg yolk and cream; then with a sharp knife score the pastry in squares or diamond shapes in the size you want to serve it, being careful not to cut through the pastry.

4. Bake for 15 to 20 minutes, being careful not to let the top get too brown. Dust with superfine sugar as soon as it comes out of the oven, and allow to cool slightly before breaking into the pieces you have marked.

⇊⇊⇊

⅄ ⅄ ⅄

CHRISTMAS DAY LUNCHEON

Oysters with Whole Wheat Bread and Lemon Wedges
Pheasant Casserole
Braised Celery
Plum Pudding with Hard Sauce
Fresh Fruits

I would be reluctant to do away with every traditional course on the Christmas menu. But at the same time I would select a menu that is not overly time-consuming. Most of my friends are worn out by the time Christmas Day arrives and have neither time nor heart for complicated cooking. If you think ahead, Plum Pudding is best made in August or September for eating in the distant future.

THE INGREDIENTS

What You Will Need:

2 medium onions
3 celery hearts
1 bunch parsley sprigs
1 lemon
Fruits
6 oysters per person
1 pheasant
1¾ pounds beef suet*
8 large eggs*

½ pound unsalted butter
¼ cup heavy cream
Sweet tomato chutney
1 1-pound loaf stale white bread*
Whole wheat bread
¾ pound currants*
¾ pound large black raisins*
¾ pound golden raisins*

Staples to Have on Hand:

salt, pepper, chicken stock (see page 276), flour, baking powder, confectioner's sugar, brandy, dry red wine

*Purchase these items only if you are preparing your own Plum Pudding. If not, buy a good quality Plum Pudding at a specialty food store.

THE WORK SCHEDULE

4 Days Before Serving

1. Check the staples on hand and make your shopping list. At this time of year allow extra time for shopping and order early to avoid disappointment and allay frustration.
2. Order oysters to be picked up on Christmas Eve. Order pheasant.
3. Plum puddings are all the better for being made 3 to 4 months in advance. On the other hand, good grocery stores will have a fine English imported pudding for sale. Next year remember to make three or four in September for use at Christmas and in January.

3 Days Before Serving

1. Select the wines and buy the fresh fruits. Store the fruits in the refrigerator securely wrapped.

2 Days Before Serving

1. Make the Hard Sauce for pudding. Store in a covered jar in the refrigerator.
2. Pick up the pheasant.

1 Day Before Serving

1. Prepare the pheasant through step 4 of the recipe. Undercook it to allow for reheating.
2. Pick up the oysters. Refrigerate until Serving Day.
3. Prepare and boil the celery hearts (steps 1 and 2 of the recipe). Drain well, cool, cover, and refrigerate.
4. Set the table and arrange fruit and flowers and gifts for guests.

Serving Day

1. If oysters are on the half shell, arrange them on a large platter for serving. I suggest thin buttered whole wheat bread and wedges of lemon as an accompaniment. If the oysters have already been shucked, ask the fishmonger to give you the shells so that you can put the oyster back on its shell. It looks so much better.

2. *Four hours before serving,* bring a pot of water to a boil for the pudding. Allow the pudding to simmer gently until you are ready for it. Keep an eye on the water level and add more as needed.

3. *Fifty minutes before serving,* preheat the oven for the pheasant and allow approximately 30 to 40 minutes for heating at 325°F.

4. Complete steps 4 and 5 of the Braised Celery recipe and heat in the same oven as the pheasant casserole. When pheasant is hot, complete the sauce and serve (steps 6 and 7 of the recipe).

5. Prepare the coffee maker and uncork the wine.

PHEASANT CASSEROLE

2 medium onions
8 tablespoons unsalted butter
1 pheasant
4 tablespoons sweet tomato chutney
1 cup dry red wine

2 cups chicken stock (see page 276)
Salt and pepper
Beurre Manié to thicken sauce (see page 282)

1. Preheat the oven to 300°F.

2. Peel and slice the onions. In a skillet, brown the onions in half the butter. Add more butter if needed, taking care the onions do not burn. Remove the onions to a casserole with a lid, one just large enough to hold the pheasant.

3. Brown the pheasant on all sides in the skillet, adding more butter if necessary. Place the pheasant on top of the onions in the casserole. Add the chutney, wine, stock, two teaspoons of salt, and a few twists of the pepper mill.

4. Bring to a boil on top of the range, then cook the casserole in the oven, covered, for 1 hour. By this time, the meat should be about to fall off the bone. Cool, cover, and refrigerate.

5. Reheat pheasant casserole in a 350°F. oven for 30 to 40 minutes. When hot remove the pheasant to a heated platter and keep warm.

6. Over low heat add the beurre manié, bit by bit, to the sauce in the casserole until the sauce reaches the desired thickness; it should resemble heavy cream. Correct the seasoning.

7. Carve the pheasant and serve the sauce from a sauceboat.

BRAISED CELERY

½ celery heart per serving or 4 celery stalks
Softened unsalted butter
Salt and pepper

¼ cup chicken stock (see page 276)
Juice of 1 lemon
Finely chopped parsley

1. Preheat the oven to 350°F.

2. Prepare the celery hearts by scraping the outside with a vegetable peeler. If celery stalks are used, treat in the same way, but cut them into 2-inch pieces on the bias.

3. Boil the celery in plenty of boiling salted water for 20 minutes. Lift out the celery and drain.

4. Butter an ovenproof dish with a cover. Arrange the hearts or stalks in the dish; dot with butter, and season lightly with salt and pepper. Pour in the chicken stock.

5. Cover and bake for 30 minutes. Before serving, sprinkle with the juice of one lemon and finely chopped parsley.

Note: Canned celery hearts can be substituted for the fresh.

⇓ ⇓ ⇓

PLUM PUDDING

1¾ pounds beef suet
1 pound white bread crumbs, made from 1 pound of stale bread
¾ pound currants
¾ pound large raisins
¾ pound golden raisins

4 cups flour
1 teaspoon baking powder
8 large eggs
½ cup brandy
¼ cup brandy for flaming
Hard Sauce (see following recipe)

1. Have ready two 24-inch squares of clean cloth.

(Continued)

2. Chill the beef suet thoroughly. Remove the membrane and grate it on the coarsest side of your grater. Prepare the bread crumbs from stale bread. Wash and dry the currants and raisins.

3. Sift the flour and baking powder together, then mix all the dry ingredients in a large bowl.

4. Beat the eggs lightly and add the one-half cup of brandy to them. Pour the egg mixture into the bowl with the dry ingredients and mix thoroughly.

5. Flour each square of cloth generously and pile half of the pudding mixture on each piece of cloth. Gather up the edges and tie them securely with heavy string.

6. Bring to a boil a pot of water large enough to hold both, or a pot for each, and boil for 5 hours. Drain the pudding and hang it up by its string. It will keep in this way for a year.

7. To serve the pudding, boil for 1 hour and unwrap from its cloth onto a serving dish. Pour warm brandy over the pudding and carry it to the table in flames, with a sprig of holly stuck in the top. Serve with Hard Sauce.

HARD SAUCE

2 cups confectioner's sugar	3 tablespoons brandy
8 tablespoons unsalted butter, softened	¼ cup heavy cream

1. Add the sugar gradually to the softened butter, using an electric beater. Mix until well blended.

2. Add the brandy and mix again. Beat in the heavy cream. Chill thoroughly before serving. This recipe makes approximately 2½ cups.

⇟ ⇟ ⇟

NEW YEAR'S EVE

Creamed Smoked Haddock
Virginia Ham and Cumberland Sauce
Lima Bean Purée
Brown Bread Ice Cream

Cod, salted or unsalted, is traditional in France on New Year's Eve, but I prefer smoked haddock—a near enough substitute to be traditional. This menu is simple, and the dessert calls for champagne with which to ring in the newborn year.

THE INGREDIENTS

What You Will Need:

½ pound small mushrooms
1 bunch parsley sprigs
1 orange
1 lemon
Virginia ham slices (2 per person)
2 pounds smoked haddock
Large eggs
¼ pound unsalted butter

1 pint heavy cream
½ cup sour cream
Milk
6 ounces whole wheat bread crumbs
3 10-ounce packages frozen baby
   lima beans
Red currant jelly

Staples to Have on Hand:

salt, pepper, cayenne, ground nutmeg, Dijon mustard, red wine vinegar, granulated sugar, vanilla extract, flour

THE WORK SCHEDULE

3 Days Before Serving

1. Check the staples on hand and make your shopping list. Complete shopping as early as possible.
2. Make Brown Bread Ice Cream. It keeps indefinitely.

2 Days Before Serving

1. Prepare the Cumberland Sauce, cover, and refrigerate.

1 Day Before Serving

1. Prepare the smoked haddock (through step 3 of the recipe). Cover the fish and the sauce and refrigerate them separately.
2. Prepare Lima Bean Purée (through step 2 of the recipe).
3. Set the table and select the wine.

Serving Day

1. *One half-hour before serving,* preheat the oven to 400°F. for smoked haddock casserole. Complete step 5 of the recipe and bake for 10 to 15 minutes, or until bubbling.
2. Unmold the Brown Bread Ice Cream onto a serving platter and put it back in the freezer.
3. Slice the ham and arrange it in an ovenproof dish. Heat it for 10 minutes in the same oven as the smoked haddock casserole.
4. Pour the Cumberland Sauce into a sauceboat. Serve at room temperature.
5. Heat the Lima Bean Purée in the top half of double boiler. It may be necessary to add a tablespoon of butter or a little heavy cream at this point.
6. Prepare the coffee maker and uncork the wines.

⇟ ⇟ ⇟

CREAMED SMOKED HADDOCK

2 pounds smoked haddock to make
   approximately 4 cups cooked and
   flaked fish
Milk, sufficient to cover fish
3 tablespoons unsalted butter

3 tablespoons flour
Ground nutmeg
Freshly ground pepper
½ pound small mushrooms

1. Soak the haddock, in enough milk to cover it, for 1 hour; then bring the haddock and milk slowly to a boil in a heavy pan. Allow it to cool. When the haddock is cool enough to handle, drain and reserve the milk. You will need 2 cups of the milk later on. Remove the haddock's skin and all the bones.

2. Make a roux by melting the butter in a heavy pan and stirring in the flour. Cook gently for 2 to 3 minutes, being careful not to burn it. Remove from the heat.

3. Heat 2 cups of the milk in which the haddock was cooked and pour it into the roux all at once. Add the nutmeg and whisk until smooth. Return to gentle heat and cook for 5 to 6 minutes, stirring all the time. Correct the seasoning with the addition of freshly ground pepper. You will find that extra salt will not be necessary. Cool, cover, and refrigerate.

4. Preheat the oven to 400°F.

5. Wipe the mushrooms clean, cutting off the stems flush with the caps. If the mushrooms are large, halve or quarter them; the pieces should be no larger than a "quarter." Add them to the sauce and cook for 2 to 3 minutes longer. Stir the sauce into the flaked fish and pile it into an ovenproof dish. Bake for 10 to 15 minutes, or until bubbling.

VIRGINIA HAM AND CUMBERLAND SAUCE

2 slices ham per serving   Cumberland Sauce (see page 281)
Dijon mustard

1. Allow two thin slices of ham rather than a thick one for each serving, and a slice above the required number will do no harm. Ham of high quality can be bought at a good delicatessen if you have not already cooked one at home; avoid the supermarket wrapped product.

2. Arrange it on a serving platter, wrap in foil, and refrigerate it until serving time.

3. Serve with Dijon mustard and Cumberland Sauce.

⇟ ⇟ ⇟

LIMA BEANS PURÉE

3 10-ounce packages frozen baby   ½ cup sour cream
   lima beans   Salt and pepper
4 tablespoons unsalted butter   Chopped parsley

1. Cook the lima beans in boiling salted water for 2 minutes. Drain.

2. Purée the beans in a food processor with the butter and sour cream. Season with salt and pepper to taste.

3. Reheat in the top half of a double boiler when needed. Garnish with chopped parsley.

⇟ ⇟ ⇟

BROWN BREAD ICE CREAM

6 ounces whole wheat bread crumbs
2 cups heavy cream
1 cup granulated sugar

½ teaspoon vanilla extract
2 tablespoons water
2 egg whites

1. Dry the bread crumbs in the oven until they are lightly browned and crisp.

2. Beat the cream until stiff, adding ¾ cup sugar gradually. Beat in the vanilla extract.

3. Simmer the remaining sugar and water together for 2 or 3 minutes. Stir into the bread crumbs and fold the mixture into the beaten cream.

4. Beat the egg whites until they hold peaks, and fold gently into the cream and crumb mixture.

5. Freeze in a 9×5-inch loaf pan (you can coat the inside of the pan with melted chocolate, if you wish) or in individual ramekins. Unmold onto a cold serving platter or cold dishes to serve.

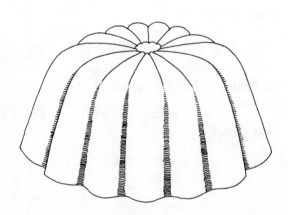

♉ ♉ ♉

EASTER

Eggs Mimosa
Jambon Persillé
Green Salad with Vinaigrette Dressing
Trifle

Tradition dictates the first two courses: eggs and parsleyed ham. The Jambon Persillé, from Burgundy, makes a spectacular showing. I could not resist including the dessert as it was prepared by my grandmother's cook.

THE INGREDIENTS

What You Will Need:

Salad greens
2 lemons
2 bunches parsley sprigs
2 or 3 branches of fresh tarragon
1 4- to 5-pound Virginia or Smith-
   field ham
1 veal knuckle, chopped
2 calves' feet, boned

2 cups chicken liver pâté or foie gras
½ dozen large or jumbo eggs
1 pint heavy cream
1 sponge cake layer
Raspberry jam
½ cup slivered almonds
2 quarts dry white wine

Staples to Have on Hand:

salt, pepper, peppercorns, bay leaf, fresh chervil, dried thyme, Dijon
mustard, white wine vinegar, red wine vinegar, olive oil, confectioner's sugar,
dry sherry

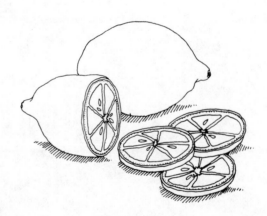

THE WORK SCHEDULE

3 Days Before Serving
1. Check the staples on hand and make your shopping list.
2. Buy everything you will need with the exception of salad greens.

2 Days Before Serving
1. Buy the salad greens.
2. Start the Jambon preparation through step 2 of the recipe. Cool, cover, and refrigerate.
3. Hardboil the eggs for the Mimosa.

1 Day Before Serving
1. Complete the Jambon Persillé (steps 3 through 5 of the recipe). Cool, cover, and refrigerate.
2. Make the mayonnaise (see page 280).
3. Make the salad dressing.
4. Set the table and select the wine.

Serving Day
1. Unmold the Jambon onto a serving dish. Refrigerate until needed.
2. *Three hours before serving,* assemble the Eggs Mimosa, but do not garnish until almost serving time. The egg yolk may be sieved and the parsley chopped in advance. Refrigerate.
3. *One or two hours before serving,* assemble and complete the trifle.
4. Arrange the salad, ready for tossing.
5. Prepare the coffee maker and uncork the wine.

⚐ ⚐ ⚐

EGGS MIMOSA

6 large or jumbo eggs, hard-boiled
   and peeled
2 cups chicken liver pâté or foie gras
1 cup heavy cream
Salt and pepper

2 cups mayonnaise (see page 280)
Lemon juice
Parsley sprigs, whole or finely
   chopped

1. Cut the eggs in half horizontally. Remove and reserve the yolks. Cut a thin slice from the bottom of each egg half so that it will stand upright.

2. Beat the pâté, adding a little cream if necessary, to make a smooth paste. Correct the seasoning with salt and pepper. Force the paste through a forcing bag, and with a large tube mound it in the egg whites. Place the filled egg halves in a serving dish.

3. Whip the cream and mix it with the mayonnaise; season with lemon juice, salt, and pepper. Spoon over the eggs.

4. Sieve the yolks and scatter them over the sauce-coated stuffed eggs. Garnish the edges of the dish with parsley.

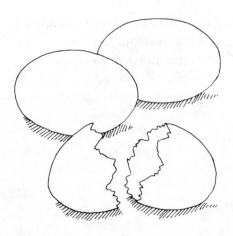

JAMBON PERSILLÉ

1 4- to 5-pound Virginia or Smith-field ham
1 veal knuckle, chopped into pieces
2 calves' feet, boned and tied to-gether
2 quarts dry white wine
Bouquet garni consisting of: 2 or 3 small branches of tarragon, a few sprigs of chervil, 1 small bay leaf, a pinch of dried thyme, 3 to 4 parsley stalks, and 10 peppercorns tied in cheesecloth
2 tablespoons white wine vinegar
1 bunch parsley, coarsely chopped

1. In a ham kettle or large pan, cover the ham with cold water and bring slowly to a boil to get rid of the excess salt. You may have to repeat the operation if the ham is very salty.

2. When the "cleansing" is complete, cover the ham once again with cold water and bring slowly to a boil. Simmer very gently for about 35 to 40 minutes. Cool, cover, and refrigerate.

3. Lift the ham out of the liquid and cut the meat off the bone in good-sized chunks. Put them in a clean pan with the knuckle of veal, calves' feet, and bouquet garni. Cover with the wine, bring to a boil, lower the heat, and simmer very gently for about an hour, skimming off the fat as it rises. The ham must be very thoroughly cooked, as it will be flaked later.

4. When you are satisfied that the ham is sufficiently cooked, pour off the liquid into a large mixing bowl through a strainer lined with three or four thicknesses of wet cheesecloth. Separate the ham from the veal and calves' feet. Stir 2 tablespoons of wine vinegar into the liquid and leave it to set slightly in the bowl or in a 4-quart mold.

5. Mash or flake the ham with a fork. It usually looks like coarse threads. Before the jelly sets, stir in the shredded ham and plenty of chopped parsley, ¾ cup at least. Pour over the ham in its bowl or mold. Stir to mix evenly. Refrigerate overnight to set.

6. To serve, turn out onto a large dish. Garnish with clumps of crisp, curly parsley. Serve with baked potatoes in their jackets.

TRIFLE

1 sponge cake layer, homemade or
   bought from a reputable baker
Raspberry jam
Good dry sherry

1 cup heavy cream, whipped
2 tablespoons confectioner's sugar
½ cup slivered almonds, toasted

   1. Cut the sponge cake into 4 × 2½-inch wedges. Split them lengthwise and spread with raspberry jam. Put the wedges together again to form sandwiches. Arrange the sandwiches in a serving bowl.

   2. Pour enough sherry over the sandwiches to saturate them completely.

   3. Beat the cream, and when soft peaks form, add the confectioner's sugar and beat again. Spoon over the soaked sponge cake, piling it high. Sprinkle with the toasted slivered almonds.

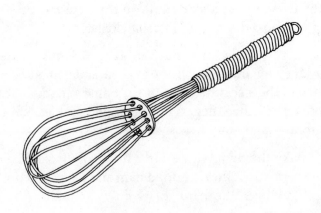

⅄ ⅄ ⅄

WEDDING BREAKFAST

Poached Salmon with Sauce Verte
Butterflied Leg of Lamb
Vegetable Mélange
St. John's Iced Lime Soufflé
Bride's Cake
Champagne

In England a wedding breakfast is served between the hours of 11 A.M. and 3 P.M. I believe the term is a throwback to the days when weddings took place at a much earlier hour, and the title of breakfast stuck.

The wedding day will have been set some time ago, leaving ample time for baking a heavy fruitcake. The icing or frosting can be done later. Royal Icing (hard and white) is suitable. It is simple to handle and in keeping with the occasion. The cake, by the way, keeps well and may be baked months before the nuptials. It should be anointed from time to time with a little cognac.

THE INGREDIENTS

What You Will Need:

2 celery stalks
1 small celery root or 2 celery stalks
4 carrots
2 small turnips
½ pound young green beans
3 small zucchini
1 onion
1 bunch parsley sprigs
2 bunches watercress
2 small bunches fresh tarragon
10 lemons
6 limes

1 8- to 10-pound salmon, cleaned
1 5-pound leg of lamb, butterflied
   and flattened
1 dozen large eggs
½ pint heavy cream
Milk
1 pound unsalted butter
1 pound currants
1 pound raisins
¾ pound ground almonds
1 envelope unflavored gelatin
Apricot jam

Staples to Have on Hand:

salt, vegetable seasoning salt, pepper, white pepper, peppercorns, bay leaf, olive oil, Dijon mustard, soy sauce, garlic clove, flour, granulated sugar, confectioner's sugar, dark brown sugar, almond extract, baking powder, green food coloring, dry white wine, cognac

THE WORK SCHEDULE

Several Months Before Serving Day
1. Bake the Bride's Cake but do not frost. Store it in an airtight tin and sprinkle it generously with cognac from time to time.

4 Days Before Serving
1. Check the staples on hand and make your shopping list.
2. Frost the Bride's Cake with Almond Icing and Royal Icing (see recipe, page 240). There is no need to refrigerate it.
3. Order the fish, lamb, and champagne.

2 Days Before Serving
1. Buy vegetables and everything else you will need.
2. Prepare the Sauce Verte, cover, and refrigerate.

1 Day Before Serving
1. Pick up the fish and lamb.
2. Prepare the Lime Soufflé and refrigerate.
3. Poach the fish and cool it in its poaching liquid. Dress by removing skin and arrange on its serving platter. Cover and refrigerate.
4. Prepare vegetables for the Mélange and cook very lightly, ready for reheating. Cover and refrigerate.
5. Set the table.

Early in the Morning of Serving Day
1. Cook the lamb but do not refrigerate. It is to be served at room temperature.
2. Chill the champagne.
3. Garnish the fish platter and arrange the lamb on a carving board.
4. *One hour before serving,* decorate the soufflé with whipped cream rosettes.
5. Place Bride's Cake where it can be seen by all.
6. Prepare coffee maker and put the champagne in a cooler.

⇊⇊⇊

POACHED SALMON

2 celery stalks, roughly chopped
2 carrots, washed and sliced
1 onion, peeled and sliced
6 to 8 parsley stalks
1 small bay leaf
8 peppercorns

4 quarts water
2 tablespoons salt
2 cups dry white wine
1 8- to 10-pound salmon, cleaned
Sauce Verte (see page 280)

1. Put the celery, carrots, onion, parsley, bay leaf, and peppercorns in a cheesecloth bag and add to the water, salt, and wine in a pan large enough to hold the fish. Bring to a boil, reduce the heat, and simmer, covered, for 30 to 40 minutes.

2. Discard the bag of aromatics and bring the court bouillon to a boil once again.

3. Measure the fish or steaks, add to the boiling court bouillon, reduce the heat, and simmer in "trembling" court bouillon for 10 minutes for each inch of thickness of the fish. Remove from the heat 5 minutes before the allotted time to allow the fish to cool in the court bouillon. When cool, cover and refrigerate. Serve with Sauce Verte.

⇟⇟⇟

BUTTERFLIED LEG OF LAMB

⅓ cup lemon juice
4 tablespoons dark brown sugar
1 clove garlic, crushed with salt
2 tablespoons Dijon mustard
2 tablespoons soy sauce

½ teaspoon salt
¼ teaspoon pepper
2 tablespoons olive oil
1 5-pound leg of lamb, butterflied and flattened

1. In a small bowl, mix together the lemon juice, brown sugar, garlic, mustard, soy sauce, salt, and pepper. Gradually add the oil.

2. One hour before cooking, brush the lamb with the sauce.

3. Preheat the oven to 475°F.

4. Put the lamb on a wire rack in a roasting pan. Roast on the highest shelf of the oven for 10 minutes a side, brushing frequently with the sauce.

5. Remove from the oven. Cool, cover, and refrigerate. Serve at room temperature, sliced thinly and on the bias, as you would a London broil.

⇓ ⇓ ⇓

VEGETABLE MÉLANGE

Unsalted butter and oil in equal quantities
2 carrots, julienned
1 small celery root, or 2 celery stalks, julienned
2 small turnips, julienned
½ pound very young green beans, topped and tailed
3 small zucchini, julienned
1 teaspoon vegetable seasoning salt
1 handful watercress leaves

1. Heat 1 tablespoon butter and 1 tablespoon oil in a wok. Add the carrots, celery root, turnips, and beans. Cook over high heat, stirring constantly. Test now and again, and as soon as the rawness begins to disappear, add the zucchini and the seasoning salt. Cook and stir for 1 or 2 minutes longer.

2. Just before serving, stir in the watercress. Serve immediately.

⇓ ⇓ ⇓

ST. JOHN'S ICED LIME SOUFFLÉ

1 envelope unflavored gelatin
¼ cup water
¾ cup milk
4 eggs, separated plus 3 additional
  whites

½ cup granulated sugar
½ cup fresh lime juice (about 6 limes)
1 cup heavy cream
3 drops of green food coloring

1. Fold over lengthwise a long strip of aluminum foil and oil it on one side. Tie it around a 1-quart soufflé dish, oiled side in, to make a collar standing 3 inches above the top.

2. Sprinkle the gelatin over the ¼ cup water to soften it. Heat the milk in the top of a double boiler.

3. Beat the egg yolks with the sugar until they are light and lemon-colored; pour the hot milk over them. Return the mixture to the top of the double boiler and add the gelatin.

4. Cook the mixture over hot water, stirring or whisking constantly, until it is thick and creamy; be careful that it does not boil. Remove the pan from the heat, let the mixture cool, then add the lime juice. Refrigerate the mixture until it begins to thicken.

5. Whip the cream until it is thick but not stiff, and fold it into the lime mixture, adding 3 drops *only* of green food coloring. Refrigerate the mixture until it is just beginning to set.

6. Beat the egg whites until they are stiff but not dry, and fold them gently into the mixture with a metal spoon. Spoon the soufflé into the prepared mold and chill it for at least 3 hours, or longer if desired. Remove collar carefully.

Variation: For those of you who live in Florida, here is a variation of St. John's Iced Lime Soufflé. In my opinion, the Key lime is a quite different fruit from the green lime that is sold by every greengrocer.

In place of ½ cup regular fresh lime juice, substitute ½ cup chilled Key lime juice (about 6 limes). Follow the directions for preparation given in the recipe for St. John's Iced Lime Soufflé. Before serving, remove the foil collar and pat ½ cup of macaroon or cake crumbs onto the sides of the soufflé.

BRIDE'S CAKE

¾ pound flour
1 teaspoon baking powder
1 pound currants
1 pound raisins
¾ pound unsalted butter
¾ pound granulated sugar

5 large eggs
1 teaspoon almond extract
4 ounces ground almonds
½ cup cognac
Almond Icing (see page 240)
Royal Icing (see page 240)

1. Preheat the oven to 325°F.

2. Line an 8½-inch springform cake pan with parchment paper.

3. Sift together the flour and baking powder. Mix the dried fruits with a little of the flour to coat them thoroughly.

4. Beat the butter until it is soft. Add the sugar gradually and beat until the butter is light in color and texture. This is best done in a mixer, but in my grandmother's day the beating was done in a large porcelain bowl with a long-handled spoon.

5. Add the eggs, one at a time, and the almond extract, beating thoroughly after each addition. Add the flour gradually while beating. Stir in the fruits and ground almonds.

6. Spoon the batter into the prepared cake pan and bake on the middle shelf of the oven for 3 to 3½ hours. If the top of cake is taking on too much color, cover it with a piece of brown paper. Test with a toothpick. If it comes out clean, the cake is done.

7. While the cake is still hot, dribble cognac over it. The cognac will soak in.

8. To complete the cake, apply Almond Icing according to instructions. Let rest for 1 hour, then spread the Royal Icing all over the cake.

ALMOND ICING

½ pound ground almonds   4 tablespoons hot water
½ pound granulated sugar   1 teaspoon almond extract
½ pound confectioner's sugar   ¼ cup apricot jam
2 large egg yolks   2 tablespoons water

1. Mix together in a small pan the almonds, the sugars, egg yolks, hot water, and almond extract. Stir over low heat until melted and combined to make a smooth paste.

2. In another small pan, heat the apricot jam and water, and cook until slightly reduced. Brush the top and sides of the cake with the jam.

3. Roll out the almond paste and fit it over the cake like a cap, pressing firmly to make it stick.

ROYAL ICING

1 cup confectioner's sugar, sifted   Juice of ½ lemon
1 large egg white

In a heavy bowl, mix the confectioner's sugar, egg white and lemon juice until smooth. Beat until the mixture is very smooth and light. It should be of such a consistency that it will not fall from the spoon. Spread with a warm damp spatula. Rough up the surface to it give a snowlike texture.

↯↯↯

BIRTHDAY PARTY

Jellied Watercress Soup
Gnocchi Parisienne with Chicken Liver Sauce
Your Favorite Green Salad with Vinaigrette Dressing
Birthday Cake

Color, flavor and texture: They are all here. Little time is needed to put all three dishes on the table, leaving ample time for the attention due the birthday person. Champagne will not be out of place with the chocolate cake.

THE INGREDIENTS

What You Will Need:

3 mushrooms
Salad greens
1 bunch watercress leaves
1 bunch parsley sprigs
1 lemon
6 chicken livers
1 dozen large eggs
½ pound unsalted butter

½ pint sour cream
½ cup heavy cream
¾ cup grated Parmesan cheese
Bovril
6 ounces semisweet chocolate
2 ounces unsweetened chocolate
¾ cup Dutch cocoa
Milk

Staples to Have on Hand:

salt, pepper, cayenne, Dijon mustard, garlic clove, baking soda, baking powder, corn syrup, vanilla extract, almond extract, tomato paste, red wine vinegar, olive oil, chicken stock (see page 276), flour, instant coffee powder, granulated sugar, dry red wine

THE WORK SCHEDULE

3 Days Before Serving

1. Check the staples on hand and make your shopping list.
2. Buy everything you will need with the exception of the watercress and salad greens.

2 Days Before Serving

1. Bake the birthday cake and, when cool, store it in an airtight container.
2. Prepare the watercress soup, cover, and refrigerate.
3. Make the Vinaigrette Dressing (see page 282), pour into screw-top jar, and refrigerate.

1 Day Before Serving

1. Buy the salad greens and watercress. Wash and dry both and store them in plastic bags in the refrigerator.
2. Prepare the gnocchi completely and the Chicken Liver Sauce (step 1 of the recipe). Spoon the sauce over the gnocchi. Cool, cover, and refrigerate.
3. Make the icing for the cake. Cover and store in the refrigerator.
4. Chill the bowls for the soup.
5. Set the table and select the wine.

Serving Day

1. Ice the cake in the afternoon, but do not refrigerate it once it has been iced.
2. *Two hours before serving*, take the gnocchi out of the refrigerator.
3. *Thirty minutes before serving*, preheat the oven to 350°F. and warm the gnocchi for 20 minutes.
4. Arrange the salad, ready for tossing.
5. Prepare the coffee maker and uncork the wine.
6. Just before serving, garnish the soup.

⇣ ⇣ ⇣

JELLIED WATERCRESS SOUP

2 cups watercress leaves, about ¾ of
  a bunch
4 cups chicken stock (see page 276)
Salt, pepper, and lemon juice to taste

Yolk of 1 hard-boiled egg, sieved, for
  garnish
Finely chopped parsley for garnish

1. Purée the watercress leaves with 1 cup of stock. Stir into remaining stock and season with salt, pepper, and lemon juice to taste.

2. Return to the refrigerator to reset.

3. To serve, spoon into cold cups. Garnish with sieved egg yolk and finely chopped parsley.

♉ ♉ ♉

GNOCCHI PARISIENNE

3 tablespoons unsalted butter
1 cup water
4 tablespoons grated Parmesan
  cheese
Salt and cayenne

½ teaspoon Dijon mustard
1 cup flour
3 eggs
Chicken Liver Sauce (see following
  recipe)

1. Melt the butter in the water with the cheese, salt and cayenne to taste, and the mustard. Bring to a boil and add the flour all at once. Remove from the heat and stir until the mixture leaves the sides of the pan.

2. Turn into a bowl and, when cooled, beat in the eggs one at a time, making sure each egg has been absorbed before the next is added.

3. With two hot, wet spoons, mold the paste into egg shapes and drop into simmering salted water. The gnocchi are done when they rise to the top. Drain on a linen towel or on paper towels.

4. To freeze, put the drained dumplings on a cookie sheet and brush each with melted butter. Freeze until hard, wrap securely, and return to the freezer.

CHICKEN LIVER SAUCE FOR GNOCCHI

6 chicken livers
1 small clove garlic
3 tablespoons unsalted butter
3 mushrooms, sliced
1 teaspoon tomato paste

1 teaspoon meat glaze (Bovril)
3 tablespoons flour
1½ cups chicken stock (see page 276)
2 tablespoons dry red wine
½ cup grated Parmesan cheese

1. Sauté the chicken livers and garlic in 2 tablespoons butter. Add the mushrooms, tomato paste, and meat glaze. Remove from the heat and blend in the flour. Add the stock and wine. Return to the heat and stir until thick. Check the seasoning—it should be very pronounced.

2. Arrange the gnocchi on the bottom of a shallow, well-buttered ovenproof dish. Sprinkle with a little grated cheese. Pour the sauce over the gnocchi and sprinkle with the remaining cheese. Dot with the remaining butter. Cool, cover, and refrigerate.

3. Preheat the oven to 350°F.

4. Bake for 20 minutes, or until hot and bubbling.

⇣⇣⇣

CHOCOLATE LAYER CAKE

¾ cup Dutch cocoa
1¾ cups granulated sugar
1 whole egg and 3 yolks (freeze remaining whites for future use)
½ cup milk
8 tablespoons unsalted butter
2 cups flour, sifted
½ teaspoon salt

1 teaspoon baking soda
1 teaspoon baking powder
1 cup sour cream
1 teaspoon vanilla extract
¼ teaspoon almond extract
Chocolate Icing (see following recipe)

(Continued)

1. Preheat the oven to 350°F.

2. Line three 8-inch baking pans with nonstick baker's paper.

3. Combine the cocoa with ¾ cup sugar, 1 egg yolk, and the milk. Cook over very low heat until the mixture is thick. Cool.

4. Cream the butter and the remaining cup of sugar until fluffy. Beat in 1 whole egg and 2 yolks.

5. Sift the flour, salt, baking soda, and baking powder together.

6. Fold in the sifted flour, sour cream, and batter, alternating one after another. Beat in the cocoa mixture, vanilla, and almond extract.

7. Pour the batter into the baking pans. Bake for 30 to 35 minutes. Do not overcook. Turn out onto racks. Spread with Chocolate Icing. Makes 3 8-inch layers.

☲ ☲ ☲

CHOCOLATE ICING

6 ounces semisweet chocolate
2 ounces unsweetened chocolate
2 tablespoons strong, prepared, instant coffee

1 teaspoon vanilla extract or rum
1 tablespoon corn syrup
½ cup heavy cream, approximately

Over low heat melt the chocolates with the coffee and vanilla or rum flavoring. Add the corn syrup. Mix well. Stir in the cream. Cool. This icing may be made ahead and frozen until needed. Yield: approximately 1½ cups.

☲ ☲ ☲

⇟⇟⇟

SUNDAY LUNCHEON

Cold Sliced Ham
Scrambled Eggs with Parsley
Pâté de Viande (Meat Loaf de Luxe)
Green Salad with Vinaigrette Dressing
Compote of Pears and Grapes
Nancy's Cookies

My editor would like to call this menu brunch, but I prefer luncheon. Ham and scrambled eggs give it the breakfast flavor, and that is the only concession I make. You can serve Bloody Marys, champagne cocktails, or white wine for a festive touch.

THE INGREDIENTS

What You Will Need:

2 onions
Small green pepper
1 bunch parsley sprigs
Salad greens
1 lemon
8 Bartlett, Comice, or Anjou pears
1 pound seedless grapes
1½ pounds Virginia ham, good boiled ham, or country ham
2 pounds ground top round or sirloin

1 pound ground veal
1 pound ground pork
1½ dozen large eggs
½ pound butter
1 cup cottage cheese
½ cup bottled chili sauce
1 8-ounce can tomato sauce
Bread crumbs
1 cup pecans
½ cup grated coconut

Staples to Have on Hand:

salt, pepper, cinnamon sticks, whole cloves, Dijon mustard, red wine vinegar, olive oil, flour, granulated sugar, brown sugar, Burgundy

⇊ ⇊ ⇊

THE WORK SCHEDULE

3 Days Before Serving
1. Check the staples on hand and make your shopping list.
2. Buy everything you will need with the exception of the salad greens and ham.

2 Days Before Serving
1. Buy the salad greens.
2. Prepare the pâté, cool, wrap securely, and refrigerate.
3. Bake Nancy's Cookies. Cool and store in an airtight container.

1 Day Before Serving
1. Buy the ham—just avoid the supermarket packaged kind. Slice the ham and arrange it on a serving platter. Wrap securely in plastic wrap and refrigerate.
2. Poach the pears (steps 1 through 3 of the recipe) and allow them to cool in their syrup. Cover and refrigerate.
3. Make the Vinaigrette Dressing (see page 282) and store in a screw-top jar in the refrigerator.
4. Set the table and select the wine.

Serving Day
1. Wash and dry the salad greens. Arrange them in a salad bowl and cover with plastic wrap. Refrigerate until serving time.
2. Garnish the pâté on its serving platter.
3. Slice the grapes and mix them with the poached pears in a glass serving bowl and refrigerate.
4. Garnish the sliced ham.
5. Prepare the eggs for scrambling (step 1 of the recipe).
6. Prepare the coffee maker.
7. Scramble the eggs and serve (step 2 of the recipe).

↓↓↓

SCRAMBLED EGGS WITH PARSLEY

6 eggs (or 1 per serving)   1 cup parsley sprigs, chopped
Salt and pepper   3 tablespoons unsalted butter

1. Break the eggs into a bowl and mix with a fork, but do not beat to a froth. Season with a little salt and pepper. Stir in the chopped parsley.

2. Melt the butter in a heavy saucepan no larger than necessary. Add the eggs and cook over low heat, stirring constantly with a wooden spoon. The eggs will cook very quickly, so be careful. They should be creamy granules. If the eggs have to wait before serving, undercook them and reheat with the addition of one more uncooked egg stirred in.

⚐ ⚐ ⚐

PÂTÉ DE VIANDE

2 pounds ground top round or sirloin   3 eggs, beaten
1 pound ground veal   3 tablespoons chopped green pep-
1 pound ground pork   per
1 cup cottage cheese   Salt and pepper
1 cup fresh bread crumbs   ½ cup Burgundy
1 cup chopped onion   1 cup tomato sauce
½ cup bottled chili sauce

1. Preheat the oven to 400°F.

2. Combine the beef, veal, and pork and mix thoroughly. Add the cottage cheese, bread crumbs, onion, chili sauce, eggs, and green pepper. Season with salt and pepper to taste. Shape into a loaf and put into a roasting pan.

3. Pour the wine over the meat loaf and spread the tomato sauce over the loaf. Bake for 30 minutes, basting frequently. Reduce the oven temperature to 350°F. and bake for 1 hour, or until done. Baste frequently as the loaf bakes. Refrigerate and serve cold.

COMPOTE OF PEARS AND GRAPES

1 cup granulated sugar
4 cups water
Juice of 1 lemon
2 cinnamon sticks

4 whole cloves
8 Bartlett, Comice, or Anjou pears
1 pound seedless grapes

1. Dissolve the sugar in the water in a saucepan with a tight-fitting lid. Add the lemon juice and spices and simmer for 10 to 15 minutes.

2. Peel and core the pears. Halve or quarter them according to your taste.

3. Put the pears carefully into the boiling syrup and poach until they test tender when pierced with a toothpick. Allow the pears to cool in the syrup. Cover and refrigerate.

4. Wash and halve the grapes. Drain the pears and mix with the grapes. Serve in a glass dish with a little of the poaching syrup.

⇓ ⇓ ⇓

NANCY'S COOKIES

BASE:
½ cup unsalted butter
1 cup flour
1 cup brown sugar

TOPPING:
½ cup brown sugar
2 eggs, beaten
1 tablespoon flour
½ cup grated coconut
1 cup pecans
Granulated sugar

1. Preheat the oven to 375°F.

2. For the base, cream the butter, flour, and brown sugar together until soft. Spread with fingers on a 11½ × 7½ × 1½-inch baking sheet and bake 15 minutes.

3. For the topping, mix carefully the ½ cup brown sugar, 2 beaten eggs, flour, and coconut. Fold in the pecans. Pour this over the previously baked layer on the baking sheet and bake for 20 minutes. Sprinkle with granulated sugar immediately after removing from the oven. Cut the biscuits while still warm, then store them in an airtight tin if they are not to be eaten right away.

⇓⇓⇓

EVENING BUFFET

Panache
Salad Argentine
Poached Striped Bass
Trifle
Pineapple with Kirsch

The evening buffet provides something for everyone: eggs (in the Panache), red meat and vegetables (in the salad), fish, a sweet dessert, and fruit for the waist watchers.

THE INGREDIENTS

What You Will Need:

1 large Spanish onion
1 onion
1 green pepper
1½ pounds plus 10 ounces green
  beans
2 celery stalks
2 carrots
4 lemons
Lettuce
1 bunch parsley sprigs
1 bunch watercress
2 ripe pineapples

2 pounds roasted sirloin of beef
1 7- to 8-pound striped bass
4 large eggs
½ pint heavy cream
2 4-ounce bottles artichoke hearts
Stuffed green olives
Pimientos
1 sponge cake layer
Raspberry jam
½ cup slivered almonds
Dry white wine

Staples to Have on Hand:

   salt, pepper, peppercorns, bay leaf, dried thyme, Dijon mustard, red wine
vinegar, olive oil, sour cream, superfine sugar, confectioner's sugar, dry
sherry, kirsch

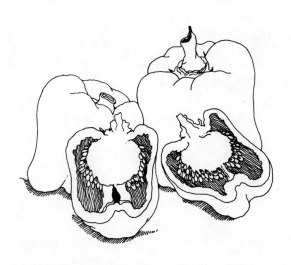

THE WORK SCHEDULE

3 Days Before Serving

1. Check the staples on hand and make your shopping list.
2. Order the fish and the beef.
3. Buy everything else you will need.

2 Days Before Serving

1. Pick up the fish and beef.
2. Roast the beef to the desired doneness (rare, medium, or well done). Cool, cover, and refrigerate.
3. Make the dressing for the Salad Argentine (step 1 of the recipe). Store in the refrigerator in a screw-top jar.
4. Prepare the Panache, but do not garnish it. Cool, cover, and refrigerate.

1 Day Before Serving

1. Cook the green beans for the Salad Argentine and dry them well. (Drying is important; it will eliminate the risk of the beans becoming soggy.) Refrigerate in a plastic bag.
2. Core and slice the pineapple. Cover and refrigerate.
3. Poach the fish and cool it in its poaching liquid. Dress it by removing the skin. Arrange the fish on its serving platter, cover, and refrigerate.
4. Decide if you will serve a sauce with the fish. If so, prepare the sauce. See recipe for suggestions.
5. Set the table and select the wine.

Serving Day

1. *Two hours before serving,* take the fish out of the refrigerator to allow it to come to room temperature.
2. *Two hours before serving,* remove the Panache from the refrigerator and garnish. Serve at room temperature.
3. *Two hours before serving,* arrange the sponge cake sandwiches in a serving bowl. Do not refrigerate.
4. *One hour before serving,* arrange the pineapple on a serving dish, sprinkle with kirsch, and return to the refrigerator.
5. *One hour before serving,* drench the sponge cake sandwiches with sherry. Whip the cream and mound it over the sandwiches. Sprinkle with toasted almonds. Do not refrigerate again.
6. Prepare the coffee maker and uncork the wine.
7. *Fifteen minutes before serving,* slice and julienne the beef and complete the Salad Argentine.

PANACHE

1 large Spanish onion
½ cup olive oil
1 green pepper
10 ounces (approximately) green beans, lightly cooked
2 4-ounce bottles of artichoke hearts, drained

4 eggs
1 teaspoon salt
¼ teaspoon pepper
Several sliced stuffed green olives for garnish
1 pimiento, cut into strips, for garnish

1. Slice the onion thinly and cook it in the olive oil until it is transparent; do not allow the onion to brown.

2. Slice and dice the pepper. Cook the beans in fast-boiling water for 5 minutes.

3. Put the beans, artichoke hearts, and onion and oil into a blender or food processor and purée. Beat the eggs to a froth and mix them with the puréed vegetables and diced green pepper. Season with salt and pepper.

4. Preheat the oven to 350°F.

5. Transfer the vegetable mixture to a well-buttered 7 × 10 × 2-inch oven-proof dish, preferably earthenware. Bake for 50 minutes. Cool, cover, and refrigerate.

6. At serving time, garnish with the olives and pimiento. Serve at room temperature.

↯↯↯

SALAD ARGENTINE

1½ tablespoons red wine vinegar	Pepper
6 tablespoons olive oil	1½ pounds cooked green beans
2 tablespoons lemon juice	2 pounds sirloin of beef, roasted,
½ teaspoon salt	sliced, and cut into julienne
4 tablespoons sour cream	Lettuce leaves
2 tablespoons Dijon mustard	Finely chopped parsley

1. Make the dressing by combing the vinegar, oil, lemon juice, salt, sour cream, mustard, and pepper to taste in a screw-top jar.

2. Mix the beans and beef with enough dressing to coat generously. Serve on lettuce leaves sprinkled with parsley.

POACHED STRIPED BASS

2 celery stalks	12 cups water
12 peppercorns	2 tablespoons salt
1 bay leaf	4 cups dry white wine
2 carrots, thinly sliced	1 7- to 8-pound striped bass
1 onion, sliced	Watercress
Pinch of dried thyme	Lemon wedges

1. To make the court bouillon, tie the celery, peppercorns, bay leaf, carrots, onion, and thyme in a cheesecloth bag. Place the bag and the other ingredients in a fish kettle. Bring to a boil and simmer for ½ hour. Discard the bag of aromatics; they have served their purpose.

2. Scrape the fish with the back of a knife to remove the scales if the fishmonger has not done this for you.

3. Place the bass on the grid and put it in the fish kettle with the gently simmering court bouillon. Simmer for about 30 minutes, or 10 minutes per inch at the thickest part of the fish. Do not allow to boil. Allow to cool sufficiently before handling.

(Continued)

4. Remove the skin and dark flesh close to the backbone. Carefully slide the fish onto a long fish platter. Garnish with watercress and lemon wedges. Serve with Sauce Verte or Sauce Tartare.

⇟⇟⇟

TRIFLE

1 sponge cake layer, homemade or
  bought from a reputable baker
Raspberry jam
Good dry sherry

1 cup heavy cream, whipped
2 tablespoons confectioner's sugar
½ cup slivered almonds, toasted

1. Cut the sponge cake into 4 × 2½-inch wedges. Split them lengthwise and spread with raspberry jam. Put the wedges together again to form sandwiches. Arrange the sandwiches in a serving bowl.

2. Pour enough sherry over the sandwiches to saturate them completely.

3. Beat the cream, and when soft peaks form, add the confectioner's sugar and beat again. Spoon over the soaked sponge cake, piling it high. Sprinkle with the toasted slivered almonds.

⇟⇟⇟

PINEAPPLE WITH KIRSCH

2 ripe pineapples
½ cup kirsch

Superfine sugar

1. Peel and core both pineapples and cut each into 8 slices. Pour the kirsch over the slices and refrigerate for at least 1 hour.

2. Serve cold, dusted with a little fine sugar.

⇟⇟⇟

COOK IT NOW, SERVE IT LATER

AFTER-THEATER SUPPER

Zucchini Rapées with Sauce Tartare
Poached Salmon with Sauce Verte
Lemon Curd and Whole Wheat Toast

For after the theater a menu should be made up of light and easy-to-serve food. This menu is both light and simple, with all the dishes ready to serve. Bread is near the toaster and is the only last-minute cooking (if you want to call it that) required.

THE INGREDIENTS

What You Will Need:

2 pounds small zucchini
2 celery stalks
2 carrots
1 onion
7 lemons
2 bunches parsley sprigs
Lettuce

1 bunch watercress
2 small bunches tarragon
1 8- to 10-pound salmon, cleaned
½ pound unsalted butter
1 dozen large eggs
Whole wheat bread

Staples to Have on Hand:

   salt, pepper, white pepper, peppercorns, bay leaves, Dijon mustard, olive oil, vegetable oil, granulated sugar, dry white wine

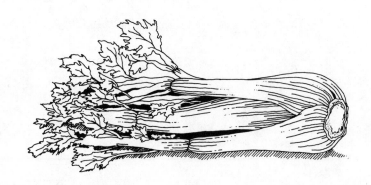

THE WORK SCHEDULE

2 Days Before Serving

1. Check the staples on hand and make your shopping list.
2. Order the salmon.
3. Buy everything else you will need.
4. Make the Lemon Curd and store in the refrigerator in a screw-top jar.

1 Day Before Serving

1. Pick up the salmon.
2. Poach the salmon, cool it in its poaching liquid, cover, and refrigerate.
3. Make the Sauce Tartare for the Zucchini Rapées (see page 279), cover, and refrigerate.
4. Make the Sauce Verte (see page 280), cover, and refrigerate.
5. Grate the zucchini, cover, and refrigerate.
6. Set the table and select the wine.

Serving Day

1. Take the salmon out of the refrigerator in the late afternoon. Arrange it on a serving platter, cover, but do not refrigerate again.
2. Arrange on lettuce leaves and sprinkle with finely chopped parsley. Leave the whole wheat bread near the toaster and the Lemon Curd in a small dish on the sideboard.
3. Just before serving, mix the grated zucchini and Sauce Tartare.
4. Prepare the coffee maker and uncork the wine.

↓↓↓

ZUCCHINI RAPÉES

6 small zucchini
Sauce Tartare (see page 279)

Lettuce leaves
Finely chopped parsley

1. Grate the zucchini into a bowl, using the coarsest side of the grater. Cover the bowl with plastic wrap to seal and refrigerate.

2. Just before serving, fold the Sauce Tartare into the zucchini. Arrange on lettuce leaves and sprinkle with finely chopped parsley.

↓↓↓

POACHED SALMON

2 celery stalks, roughly chopped
2 carrots, washed and sliced
1 onion, peeled and sliced
6 to 8 parsley stalks
1 small bay leaf
8 peppercorns

4 quarts water
2 tablespoons salt
2 cups dry white wine
1 8- to 10-pound salmon, cleaned
Sauce Verte (see page 280)

1. Put the celery, carrots, onion, parsley, bay leaf, and peppercorns in a cheesecloth bag and add to the water, salt, and wine in a pan large enough to hold the fish. Bring to a boil, reduce the heat, and simmer, covered, for 30 to 40 minutes.

2. Discard the bag of aromatics and bring the court bouillon to a boil once again.

3. Measure the fish or steaks, add to the boiling court bouillon, reduce the heat, and simmer in "trembling" court bouillon for 10 minutes for each inch of thickness of the fish. Remove from the heat 5 minutes before the allotted time to allow the fish to cool in the court bouillon. When cool, cover and refrigerate. Serve with Sauce Verte.

LEMON CURD

1 stick (4 ounces) unsalted butter
½ cup granulated sugar
4 egg yolks
1 egg

Juice of 4 lemons
Grated peel of 3 lemons
Whole wheat toast

1. Melt the butter and dissolve the sugar in the top of a double boiler over gently simmering water.

2. Blend the egg yolks and egg thoroughly. Add the eggs, lemon juice, and grated lemon peel to the sugar and butter and cook, stirring now and again, until heavy and thick.

3. Cool and store in screw-top jars. It will keep for two weeks in the refrigerator.

4. To serve, spread the Lemon Curd on whole wheat toast.

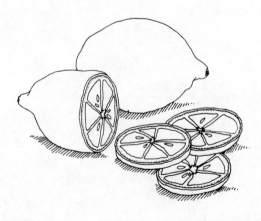

⇵⇵⇵

SUMMER BUFFET

Indian River Soup
Vitello Tonnato
Strawberries Escoffier

   This is my favorite cold menu for sultry summer days. It is equally welcome either for a luncheon or for an evening buffet, and is particularly attractive if served in a garden or on a terrace. One of its chief attractions is the very short time it takes to put together. The wine you serve with it might be rosé from Provence or, if you are fortunate enough to track it down, the Onion Skin, "Pelure d'Oignon" from the region west of Marseilles.

THE INGREDIENTS

What You Will Need:

3 carrots
4 celery stalks
1 medium onion
1 large onion
1 bunch parsley sprigs
2 lemons
3 large oranges
2 pints strawberries
3- to 4-pound piece of boneless veal,
   cut from the leg and tied with
   string

1 7-ounce can tuna fish in oil
1 small can anchovy fillets
2 large eggs
Heavy cream
1 1-pound can Italian plum tomatoes with basil
Cooked rice
Dry white wine

Staples to Have on Hand:

   salt, pepper, white pepper, peppercorns, bay leaf, capers, garlic cloves, sour
pickles, granulated sugar, chicken stock (see page 276), Grand Marnier, dry
vermouth

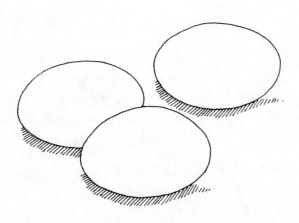

THE WORK SCHEDULE

3 Days Before Serving

1. Check the staples on hand and make your shopping list.
2. Buy everything you will need with the exception of the strawberries.
3. Order the veal.

2 Days Before Serving

1. Buy the veal.
2. Prepare the soup; cool, cover, and refrigerate.
3. Begin the preparation of the Vitello Tonnato (through step 2 of the recipe). Allow the veal to cool in the liquid. Cover and refrigerate.
4. Make the syrup for the strawberries. Cool, cover, and refrigerate.

1 Day Before Serving

1. Buy the strawberries.
2. Lift the veal out of the liquid, wrap it in plastic wrap or foil, and refrigerate. Reduce the veal liquid over high heat until only 2 to 2½ cups remain. Strain, discard the solids, cover and refrigerate (step 2 of the recipe).
3. If you are preparing homemade mayonnaise for the Vitello Tonnato, make it today (see page 280).
4. Boil the rice, drain, and refrigerate in a covered plastic container.
5. Boil the eggs for the Vitello Tonnato.
6. Chill the bowls for the soup.
7. Set the table and select the wine.

Serving Day

1. Slice the veal, cover, and refrigerate until two hours before serving.
2. Prepare the sauce for the veal (step 4 of the recipe).
3. Wash, hull, and dry the strawberries. Put them in their serving bowl and pour the sauce over them. Do not refrigerate.
4. *Two hours before serving,* assemble the veal dish (step 5 of the recipe), but do not garnish with the egg yolk and parsley until the last minute (step 6).
5. Prepare the coffee maker and uncork the wine.
6. *Just before serving,* garnish the soup.

INDIAN RIVER SOUP

1 1-pound can Italian plum tomatoes with basil included
1 carrot, shredded
½ medium onion, chopped
1 bay leaf
Peel of 1 lemon, grated
6 peppercorns
3 cups chicken stock (see page 276)

2 tablespoons sugar
½ cup dry vermouth
Salt and freshly ground pepper
(preferably white)
Peel of 1 orange
Juice of 1 orange
½ cup parsley, finely chopped

1. In a heavy 2-quart pan bring the tomatoes, carrot, onion, bay leaf, lemon peel, and peppercorns to a boil, then simmer very gently for 8 minutes.

2. Strain carefully into a clean pan. Discard the solids. Stir in the chicken stock.

3. Place the soup over moderate heat and add the sugar and vermouth. Continue heating almost to the boiling point, then remove from the heat. Season with salt and freshly ground pepper to taste. Proceed cautiously with the pepper.

4. Meanwhile, peel the orange very carefully, avoiding the white pith; cut the peel into very thin strips ½ inch long. Put the peel aside to be used as a garnish. Squeeze the orange and strain, adding the juice to the soup. The soup can be served cold at this point.

5. To serve hot, reheat the soup gently. Ladle the soup into bowls or soup plates and sprinkle with finely chopped parsley and the orange rind.

VITELLO TONNATO

3- to 4-pound boneless piece of solid veal, cut from the leg, tied with string
1 7-ounce can tuna fish in oil
1 small can anchovy fillets
2 cups dry white wine
½ sour pickle, coarsely chopped
2 carrots
1 large onion
4 stalks celery

2 cloves garlic
8 peppercorns
4 to 5 sprigs parsley
Mayonnaise (see page 280)
Lemon juice
Cooked rice
2 tablespoons capers
Yolks of 2 hard-boiled eggs
Finely chopped parsley

1. Place the veal in a large, heavy saucepan with water barely to cover.

2. Drain and flake the tuna. Drain the anchovy fillets and chop coarsely. Add both to the saucepan. Add the wine and the pickle. Coarsely chop the carrots, onion, celery, and garlic and tie in a piece of cheesecloth with the peppercorns, and the parsley. Add to the pan, and bring the liquid to a boil. Lower heat to simmer and cook for 1½ hours. Remove from the heat and cool the veal in the stock. Remove the veal, cut off the strings, and set aside. Remove the cheesecloth bag and discard.

3. Place the saucepan of stock over high heat and reduce the liquid by boiling rapidly to about 2 cups of strong stock. Strain the stock through several layers of cheesecloth into a mixing bowl and allow to cool. Refrigerate until it becomes jelly.

4. Stir sufficient mayonnaise into the jellied stock to make a heavy masking sauce. Season to taste with lemon juice.

5. Cut the veal into ¼-inch-thick slices. Make a mound of your favorite cooked rice on a large serving platter and cover the rice with the sliced veal. Spoon the sauce over the veal slices. Scatter the capers on top.

6. Press the egg yolks through a fine sieve. Sprinkle a border of finely chopped parsley around the edge of the dish, and inside of that a border of sieved egg yolk.

STRAWBERRIES ESCOFFIER

2 pints strawberries
2 large oranges
4 tablespoons granulated sugar

⅓ cup Grand Marnier
Whipped cream

1. Wash and hull the strawberries. Drain.

2. Grate the orange peels, taking care not to include any of the white pith.

3. In a sturdy bowl, pound the sugar with the grated peel.

4. Squeeze the juice from the oranges and pour it over the peel and sugar. Stir well and add the Grand Marnier.

5. Pour the syrup over the strawberries and mix well. Allow to macerate for at least 1 hour. (The flavor will be more pronounced if the fruit is not refrigerated.) Serve with whipped cream.

⇟⇟⇟

A PICNIC

Carrots Rapées
Virginia Baked Chicken
Chocolate Truffles
Fresh Fruits

Ants and dried-out, curled-at-the-edge sandwiches have been the ingredients of many picnics I have been invited to attend. With this menu I get away from all that.

Equipment has been cut to the bare minimum. Heavy paper plates, forks, glasses for wine, and cups for coffee are all that are needed. Baked chicken, truffles, and fruit are finger foods, so provide plenty of paper napkins.

THE INGREDIENTS

What You Will Need:

Carrots (for quantity, see Note,
  page 273)
1 bunch parsley sprigs
Fruits
1 broiling chicken

¾ pound unsalted butter
½ dozen large eggs
½ pint sour cream
1 pound semisweet chocolate
Bread crumbs

Staples to Have on Hand:

   salt, white pepper, red wine vinegar, vegetable oil, olive oil, cocoa powder,
granulated sugar, confectioner's sugar, dark rum

THE WORK SCHEDULE

2 Days Before the Picnic

1. Check the staples on hand and make your shopping list.
2. Buy everything you will need.
3. Make the Chocolate Truffles. Store them in an airtight container in the refrigerator.

1 Day Before the Picnic

1. Bake the chicken and arrange it in a suitable container. Refrigerate until it is time to leave for the picnic. It is better when eaten at room temperature, so by the time you get to your picnic site, it should be perfect.
2. Grate the carrots for the Rapée into a bowl. Cover the bowl with plastic wrap and refrigerate.
3. Make the dressing for the carrots in a screw-top jar (step 2 of the recipe) and refrigerate. Toss the salad at the picnic.

Picnic Day

1. Pack carefully, checking each item against your list to be sure you don't forget anything you need.

CARROTS RAPÉES

Carrots
¼ cup red wine vinegar
¼ teaspoon salt
½ teaspoon granulated sugar (optional)
¼ teaspoon white pepper
½ cup vegetable oil
½ cup olive oil
2 tablespoons finely chopped parsley

1. Grate the carrots on the coarsest side of a grater or put them through the coarsest disc of a food processor. Cover and refrigerate until needed.

2. Combine the vinegar, salt, sugar, pepper, and the oils in a screw-top jar. Shake just before pouring over the carrots. Toss the dressing and the carrots together and sprinkle with parsley just before serving.

Note: The number of carrots needed will depend on their size; choose small when possible. The dressing will coat 6 to 8 servings.

⇟ ⇟ ⇟

VIRGINIA BAKED CHICKEN

1 broiling chicken, cut into 8 pieces
1 cup sour cream
½ cup seasoned bread crumbs (see
   Note)
Melted butter

1. Preheat the oven to 375°F.

2. Skin the chicken pieces and put them in a shallow dish. Cover each piece completely with sour cream.

3. Lift the chicken pieces from the sour cream one by one and roll in the bread crumbs. As each piece is crumbed, place it on an oiled baking sheet.

4. Dribble the melted butter over each piece of chicken and bake for 45 minutes.

Note: If you prefer to make your own seasoned bread crumbs, you can add 1 teaspoon salt, ¼ teaspoon pepper, and 1 teaspoon dried thyme to 2 cups of bread crumbs.

CHOCOLATE TRUFFLES

1 pound semisweet chocolate   6 tablespoons dark rum
½ pound unsalted butter, softened   ¾ cup cocoa powder
6 egg yolks   ¾ cup confectioner's sugar

Melt the chocolate over simmering water. Beat in the butter, egg yolks, and rum with a whisk until the mixture is workable and can be shaped into round balls 1 inch in diameter. Roll the truffles in cocoa and confectioner's sugar. Put into an airtight container and refrigerate. Makes 80 to 90 pieces.

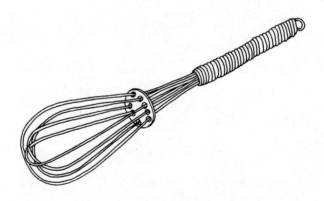

⇓⇓⇓

STOCKS, SAUCES, AND DRESSINGS

BEEF STOCK

6 pounds shin and marrow bones,
  cut into pieces
16 cups cold water
8 peppercorns
6 whole cloves
1 bay leaf
1 teaspoon dried thyme

3 parsley sprigs
1 large carrot, diced
3 celery stalks, diced
1 cup canned or fresh tomatoes,
  drained
1 medium onion, diced
1 small white turnip, diced

1. Preheat the oven to 450°F.

2. Put the bones in a roasting pan and brown them in the oven.

3. Put the browned bones in a large stockpot with the water and bring to a boil slowly. Reduce the heat and simmer, uncovered, for 30 minutes.

4. Remove the scum from the top of the stock and add the remaining ingredients. Bring to a boil, reduce the heat, and simmer, partially covered, for 6 hours.

5. Strain the stock and discard the solids. Cool uncovered, and refrigerate uncovered. Remove the fat when the stock is cold. The degreased stock may be frozen.

⇓⇓⇓

CHICKEN STOCK

4 pounds chicken backs, necks, wings, and feet
16 cups cold water
8 white peppercorns
1 bay leaf
1 teaspoon dried thyme

6 whole cloves
6 parsley stalks
1 medium onion, diced
3 stalks celery, diced
1 medium carrot, diced

Combine all the ingredients in a large stockpot and bring to a boil. Reduce the heat and simmer for 2½ to 3 hours, or until reduced by half. Skim off the scum as it rises to the top. Strain the stock and discard the solids. Cool uncovered, and refrigerate uncovered. Remove the fat when the stock is cold. The degreased stock may be frozen.

⇟ ⇟ ⇟

VEAL STOCK

2½ to 3 pounds veal bones
1 carrot
1 celery stalk
1 small onion, peeled

1 bay leaf
A few peppercorns
Salt to taste

1. Put all the ingredients in a large pan and cover them by 2 or 3 inches of cold water. Bring to a boil and simmer for 3 to 4 hours, skimming the scum from the top.

2. Strain the stock and discard the solids. The stock freezes very well.

⇟ ⇟ ⇟

FISH STOCK

2 pounds bones and head of white fish	2 small bay leaves
2 celery stalks, coarsely chopped	1 tablespoon salt
1 large onion, unpeeled and chopped	8 cups cold water
2 small carrots, washed and chopped	2 cups dry white wine
	6 peppercorns

Put all the ingredients, except the peppercorns, in a large enameled or steel-lined pan. Bring to a boil, reduce the heat, and cook uncovered. Skim frequently until no more scum rises. Add the peppercorns and simmer gently for 2 hours. Strain, cool, and refrigerate. The stock can be frozen.

⇟ ⇟ ⇟

BROWN SAUCE

⅓ cup finely chopped carrot	6 cups beef stock (see page 275)
⅓ cup finely chopped onion	2 tablespoons tomato paste
⅓ cup finely chopped celery	8 peppercorns
6 tablespoons oil, bacon fat, or clarified butter	1 small bunch parsley
½ cup chopped lean bacon or ham	1 bay leaf
4 tablespoons flour	Salt and pepper

1. In a heavy 2-quart saucepan, cook the vegetables with the oil and bacon for 15 minutes. Stir in the flour and cook slowly for 8 to 10 minutes, or until the flour browns.

2. Remove from the heat, pour in the beef stock, and blend with a wire whisk. Stir in the tomato paste, peppercorns, parsley, and bay leaf.

3. Simmer slowly for 2 hours or longer. Season with salt and pepper to taste and strain, discarding the solids. Makes about 2 cups.

MADEIRA SAUCE

2 cups Brown Sauce (see page 277)   ¼ cup Madeira

Combine the ingredients and simmer for 5 minutes.

⇟ ⇟ ⇟

BÉCHAMEL SAUCE

2 cups milk   2 tablespoons unsalted butter
2 onion slices   2 tablespoons flour
1 small bay leaf   Salt
12 peppercorns

1. Combine the milk, onion, bay leaf, and peppercorns in a saucepan. Cover and simmer gently for 5 to 6 minutes. Strain through a sieve into a bowl and discard the onion and spices.

2. Melt the butter in a heavy saucepan and add the flour. Cook and stir for 5 minutes, making sure that it does not burn.

3. Add half of the strained warm milk to the roux, mix thoroughly, then add the remaining milk. Boil quickly for 2 minutes. Season with salt to taste.

⇟ ⇟ ⇟

MORNAY SAUCE

¼ to ½ cup grated Parmesan and   2 cups Béchamel Sauce (see page 278)
Gruyère cheese, in equal amounts

Stir the grated cheese into the hot Béchamel Sauce. If the sauce is to be used for coating, reduce the quantity of cheese used.

HOLLANDAISE SAUCE

4 egg yolks
2 tablespoons lemon juice
¼ teaspoon salt

Pinch of cayenne
8 tablespoons boiling unsalted butter

Put all the ingredients except the butter in a blender and give it a few turns at low speed. Immediately remove the blender cover and add the butter in a steady stream, blending well.

SAUCE TARTARE

2 hard-boiled eggs
2 egg yolks
1 tablespoon Dijon mustard
¼ teaspoon salt
1 cup oil

3 tablespoons minced sour pickle
3 to 4 tablespoons minced capers
3 to 4 tablespoons minced parsley,
  chives, or tarragon
Lemon juice

1. Sieve the yolks of the hard-boiled eggs and chop the whites coarsely.

2. In a bowl, mix the sieved and raw yolks with the mustard and salt. Using an electric beater at slow speed, add the oil drop by drop to begin with. When the oil is being absorbed, the mixture will become creamy.

3. Pour the remainder of the oil in slowly while continuing to beat. Stir in the pickle, capers, and herbs. Add lemon juice to taste. Stir in the chopped egg whites and mix well.

MAYONNAISE

2 egg yolks
¼ teaspoon Dijon mustard
Salt and pepper

1 to 1½ cups olive oil, approximately
1 tablespoon lemon juice or wine
vinegar, approximately

1. Set a mixing bowl on a wet towel. Add the egg yolks, mustard, and a pinch of salt and pepper to the bowl. Beat with a wooden spoon or whisk. Add about 2 tablespoons of the oil, a drop at a time. Whisk.

2. When the oil is absorbed, gradually add the remaining oil while stirring. Make sure all the oil is absorbed before you add more. If the mixture is too thick, add a little lemon juice or vinegar. Correct the seasonings by adding more salt, pepper, and lemon juice or vinegar.

SAUCE VERTE

1 bunch watercress
2 cups parsley, tightly packed
2 small bunches fresh tarragon

2 cups mayonnaise (see following
recipe)
2 tablespoons lemon juice
White pepper (optional)

1. Trim off the stalks of the watercress and use only the fresh leaves. Break off the heads of the parsley and strip the coarse stalks from the tarragon. Wash the greens thoroughly and drain well until they are free of moisture.

2. Combine the mayonnaise and greens in a blender and mix at high speed. Add the lemon juice and the white pepper, if desired.

CUMBERLAND SAUCE

1 lemon
1 orange
¼ cup water
¼ cup port wine
½ tablespoon Dijon mustard

1 tablespoon red wine vinegar
2 heaping tablespoons red currant jelly
Salt and cayenne

1. Peel the lemon and orange very thinly, making sure you do not take off any of the white pith. Cut the peels into very thin shreds and simmer in ¼ cup water for 5 minutes. Drain and set aside.

2. Squeeze the lemon and orange and put the juices into a small pan with the wine, mustard, vinegar, jelly, and salt and cayenne to taste. Simmer over low heat for 5 minutes. Cool and store in a screw-top jar in the refrigerator. The sauce keeps well.

⇓ ⇓ ⇓

CRANBERRY-CUMBERLAND SAUCE

2 oranges
1 to 1½ cups water
½ cup red currant jelly
½ cup light port wine
1½ to 2 cups granulated sugar

2 cinnamon sticks
¼ teaspoon whole allspice
2 cups fresh cranberries, picked over and washed

1. Cut the peel of 1 orange into fine strips. Simmer in the water for 2 to 3 minutes and drain.

2. Combine the juice of both oranges, the jelly, wine, and sugar with the cinnamon sticks and allspice tied in a cheesecloth bag. Bring to a boil and simmer for 5 minutes.

3. Remove the spice bag and add the cranberries and orange peel to the syrup. Bring to a full rolling boil until the berries pop.

4. Cool and serve at room temperature.

SAUCE SCANDIA

1 tablespoon Dijon mustard
1 tablespoon granulated sugar
1½ tablespoons red wine vinegar
½ teaspoon salt

Pinch of white pepper
1 teaspoon lemon juice
1 tablespoon chopped fresh dill
4 tablespoons vegetable oil

Combine all the ingredients in a screw-top jar and shake well. Allow to stand for several hours before using. If you have a sweet tooth, add more sugar.

VINAIGRETTE DRESSING

2 tablespoons red wine vinegar
8 tablespoons olive oil
1 teaspoon Dijon mustard

1 teaspoon lemon juice
1 teaspoon salt
Pepper to taste

Combine all the ingredients in a screw-top jar and mix well.

CLARIFIED BUTTER

Put ½ pound unsalted butter in a heavy pan and heat gently. Remove the scum and strain the clear fat into a clean container. Cover and refrigerate.

BEURRE MANIÉ

Blend equal parts of flour and unsalted butter and roll into balls of about 1 teaspoon each. Wrap separately and freeze for future use.

MINT BUTTER

8 tablespoons unsalted butter, softened
2 large handfuls fresh mint leaves
1 teaspoon salt

2 to 3 twists of the pepper mill
Sugar
Lemon juice

1. Purée the butter and mint leaves in a food mill or blender. Season the mixture with salt, pepper, sugar and lemon juice to taste.

2. Chill and roll into sausage-shape portions. Freeze until needed.

↓↓↓

SELECTING THE WINE

In a recent learned paper on wines I read that there is a growing interest in serving light red wines with chicken, turkey, and other poultry. This information is refreshing—refreshing to know that at long last the hard and fast rule governing wine choice is being ignored. To be told that white wines should be served with white meats and reds with red meat is like telling someone that only a black tie should be worn on Sunday. I never could see what color had to do with it—after all, what if you were color blind? It is the palate that counts, and it is the palate that should be pampered.

For as long as I can remember I have been serving "reds" with roast chicken and turkey and have found the marriage a comfortable one. My very unprofessional advice is to drink what pleases you with what you are eating, and very soon you will find out what goes with what. Read about wine and listen to the experts, but don't necessarily follow their advice to the bitter end. Learn from them, and very soon your horizon will be broader and you will be in a position to judge for yourself. Avoid the wine snobs and buffs who confuse with unintelligible language and those who lay down rigid rules. Brian St. Pierre, a noted wine authority, warns that you will find many self-appointed experts who insist that only one wine from a particular vineyard in a special year goes with a particular dish. Such restrictions are totally unnecessary. I wholeheartedly agree with Mr. St. Pierre.

Ever since my first visit to America in 1946 I have been a champion of California wines. For many years it was virtually impossible to find them in restaurants on the east coast, and were you to ask the wine waiter for the California wine list he would look at you as if your request were indecent. All that has changed, and the strides that have been made since 1946 are startling. We know about and appreciate the quality of wines produced in this country and are no longer afraid to order them. The prophet is at last honored in his own country. The Wine Institute of California gives the amateur excellent advice on serving wine. I will quote some of their suggestions for selecting wines:

BEEF   Cabernet Sauvignon, Pinot Noir, Barbera, Ruby Cabernet, or California Burgundy.

LAMB   Cabernet Sauvignon, Zinfandel, or Gamay Beaujolais.

PORK   Rosé or a sturdy white like Chardonnay or Pinot Blanc. Also, light reds like Zinfandel or Gamay Beaujolais. (The latter would be my personal choice.)

VEAL   Chardonnay if veal is breaded or sautéed. If the meat is sauced, stewed, or prepared in any of the Italian styles, robust reds like Petite Sirah or Barbera.

HAM   Grenache Rosé, Gamay Rosé, California Vin Rosé or dry Champagne.

CHICKEN   Lighter wines such as Johannisberg Riesling, Emerald Riesling, Chenin Blanc, Grey Riesling, or California Chablis.

TURKEY   Lighter wines as for chicken, Johannisberg Riesling, Emerald Riesling, Chenin Blanc, Grey Riesling, California Chablis, or a Gewürztraminer.

DUCK AND For all dark, flavorful meat, select Pinot Noir, Gamay
GOOSE   Beaujolais, or Zinfandel.

FISH AND Full-flavor whites, such as Chardonnay, Fume Blanc,
SHELLFISH Sauvignon Blanc, Pinot Blanc, or Dry Semillon.

This is a guide and not a gospel. Explore and experiment, and remember the words of Benjamin Franklin who wrote in his infinite wisdom: "Wine is proof that God loves us and wants to see us happy."

WEIGHTS, MEASURES, AND METRIC CONVERSIONS

WEIGHTS AND MEASURES:

A pinch = amount that can be picked up between finger and thumb
1 teaspoon = ⅓ tablespoon
1 tablespoon = 3 teaspoons
2 tablespoons = ⅛ cup or 1 fluid ounce
4 tablespoons = ¼ cup or 2 ounces
5⅓ tablespoons = ⅓ cup or 2⅔ ounces
8 tablespoons = ½ cup or 4 ounces
16 tablespoons = 1 cup or 8 ounces
¼ cup = 4 tablespoons
⅜ cup = 5 tablespoons or ¼ cup plus 2 tablespoons
⅝ cup = 10 tablespoons or ½ cup plus 2 tablespoons
⅞ cup = ¾ cup plus 2 tablespoons
1 cup = ½ pint or 8 fluid ounces
2 cups = 1 pint or 16 fluid ounces
2 pints = 1 quart, liquid, or 4 cups
4 quarts = 1 gallon, liquid
8 dry quarts = 1 peck
4 pecks = 1 bushel
1 pound = 16 ounces

METRIC CONVERSION TABLE:

DRY INGREDIENTS

Ounces to Grams:

Ounces	Grams	Ounces	Grams
1	28.35	9	255.15
2	56.70	10	283.50
3	85.05	11	311.85
4	113.40	12	340.20
5	141.75	13	368.55
6	170.10	14	396.90
7	198.45	15	425.25
8	226.80	16	453.60

Grams to Ounces:

Grams	Ounces	Grams	Ounces
1	0.03	9	0.32
2	0.07	10	0.35
3	0.11	11	0.39
4	0.14	12	0.42
5	0.18	13	0.46
6	0.21	14	0.49
7	0.25	15	0.53
8	0.28	16	0.57

Pounds to Kilograms: / *Kilograms to Pounds:*

Pounds	Kilograms	Kilograms	Pounds
1	0.45	1	2.205
2	0.91	2	4.41
3	1.36	3	6.61
4	1.81	4	8.82
5	2.27	5	11.02

LIQUID INGREDIENTS

Liquid Ounces to Milliliters:

Liquid Ounces	Milliliters	Liquid Ounces	Milliliters
1	29.57	6	177.44
2	59.15	7	207.02
3	88.72	8	236.59
4	118.30	9	266.16
5	147.87	10	295.73

Milliliters to Liquid Ounces:

Milliliters	Liquid Ounces	Milliliters	Liquid Ounces
1	0.03	6	0.20
2	0.07	7	0.24
3	0.10	8	0.27
4	0.14	9	0.30
5	0.17	10	0.33

Quarts to Liters: / *Liters to Quarts:*

Quarts	Liters	Liters	Quarts
1	0.95	1	1.06
2	1.89	2	2.11
3	2.84	3	3.17
4	3.79	4	4.23
5	4.73	5	5.28

Gallons to Liters: / *Liters to Gallons:*

Gallons	Liters	Liters	Gallons
1	3.78	1	0.26
2	7.57	2	0.53
3	11.36	3	0.79
4	15.14	4	1.06
5	18.93	5	1.32

↓↓↓

INDEX

A

F

lime
  sorbet, 88
  soufflé, 238
orange(s)
  ananas glacés, 70
  and cracked caramel, 116
  soufflé, Valerie's cold, 141
peach frappé, 63, 206
pear(s)
  and grape compote, 152, 251
  poires noires, 197-98
  and strawberry compote, 146
picnic, 270
pineapple with kirsch, 192, 258
Sabayon frappé aux pêches, 63, 206
sorbet, lime, 88
strawberry(ies)
  Escoffier, 159, 269
  and pear compote, 146
Valerie's cold orange soufflé, 141

G

Garlic sausage (saucisson en brioche), 158
Gnocchi Parisienne, 196, 244
  chicken liver sauce for, 197, 245
Goose, wine with, 287
Grapes, compote of pears and, 152, 251
Green beans
  haricots verts, 87-88
  in panache, 44, 256
Green olives, chicken breasts with, 81
Green salad, simple, 33
Grunt, blueberry, 105

H

Haddock, smoked
  creamed, 169, 224

Muscatel, 126
Ham
  cold sliced, 247
  entrées, 164, 170, 225, 231
  jambon persillé, 164, 231
  mousse, 98
  Virginia, and Cumberland sauce, 170, 225
  wine with, 286
Hard sauce, 220
Haricots verts, 87-88
Hollandaise sauce, 279

I

Ice, tomato, 50
Ice cream
  brown bread, 34, 226
  meringues filled with, 93-94
Icings
  almond, 240
  chocolate, 246
  royal, 240
Indian river soup, 267

J

Jambon persillé, 164, 231
Jellied watercress soup, 196, 244
July Fourth menu, 201-6

K

Kirsch, pineapple with, 192, 258
Kitchen equipment, 16-17